PAUL E. BARTON is Vice President for Planning and Policy Development at the National Institute for Work and Learning. A graduate of Princeton University, he joined the Policy Planning Staff of the Department of Labor (later Office of Policy Planning and Research) where he specialized in such areas as employment and training policy and vocational education. He has published numerous papers and articles on adult education and related subjects.

D1383186

Worklife Transitions

WORKLIFE TRANSITIONS

The Adult Learning Connection

PAUL BARTON

and The National Institute for Work and Learning

Foreword by Willard Wirtz

McGRAW-HILL BOOK COMPANY

New York   St. Louis   San Francisco
Auckland   Bogotá   Hamburg   Johannesburg   London   Madrid
Mexico   Montreal   New Delhi   Panama   Paris   São Paulo
Singapore   Sydney   Tokyo   Toronto

ISBN 0-07-003974-7

Thomas H. Quinn and Michael Hennelly were the editors of this book. Christopher Simon was the designer. Teresa F. Leaden supervised the production. It was set in Times Roman by Datapage, Inc.

Printed and bound by R. R. Donnelley and Sons, Inc.

LIBRARY OF CONGRESS CATALOGING IN PUBLICATION DATA

Barton, Paul E.
  Worklife transitions.

  Bibliography: p.
  Includes index.
  1. Continuing education. 2. Industry and education.
I. National Institute for Work and Learning (U.S.)
II. Title.
LC5219.B35   374   81-8331

                                                                    AACR2

1 2 3 4 5 6 7 8 9 0 DODO 8 9 8 7 6 5 4 3 2 1

Contents

Foreword

It is uncommon advocacy that pays such respect to its ultimate purpose that it chooses carefully among the available arguments and contributes as much to understanding as to persuasion. Paul Barton and his associates are unquestionably committed strongly and deeply to expanding substantially the opportunities in this country for adult education. Yet they prove no less intent on seeing this come about for the right reasons, and they have produced in consequence not only a convincing but a thought-provoking document.

This emerges particularly in the handling here of the two sets of values "adult education" serves. One involves the significance of occupationally oriented retraining programs to employers greatly concerned right now about productivity and to an economy shifting rapidly from a production to a service base. There are, in addition, the individual human values: the meaning of continuing retraining and broader educational renewal opportunities not only to employees whose jobs and careers come into jeopardy but to all of us who realize that "progress" is moving so fast now that we know and understand less of the whole every passing day of our lives.

The most obvious and easiest handling of these two sets of values would be to rely for recommendation of adult education's enlargement on both of them. In a sense and to a limited degree this is done here. The two value themes are developed throughout most of these chapters in a subtle, sensitive point and counterpoint.

What is more notable, though, is the consistently predominant emphasis on what are essentially the human values involved here. The concentration is on what the accelerating transition factor is coming to mean in individuals' lives. The "worklife" phrase is used broadly. The "learning connection" is becoming critical not only to established workers threatened or displaced by robots or new directions the economy may be taking, but to women wanting to move from career motherhood to career something else, and to older people at the pass between careers and not much at all. What comes through here more clearly than it has been marked out before is that in millions of Americans' lives retraining or a return to formal learning is a determinative difference between a reprieve of opportunity and a lifetime sentence to frustration, meaninglessness, obsolescence.

The economy values theme keeps coming up primarily in terms of there being sufficient "bottom line" value to employers to warrant investment in their employees' improving themselves, both by enhancing their skills and widening their broader learning base. Indeed it is only at the end, that the author and his colleagues note at all strongly that the principal motive force behind adult education may well emerge from the dependence on the "learning connection" of an economy that is itself in extraordinary transition.

Wondering about the reasons for this constraint, I come to two possibilities, and back to renewed respect for these advocates' insistence that what is involved here is too important to warrant superficial or careless persuasion.

First, we still know comparatively little about the actual relationship between broadening the educational or learning base of the work force and making the economy work better. .

No one questions the proposition that better educated and more highly skilled employees can and probably will be more productive. What we don't know, though, is how important this employee factor is in the obviously broader productivity equation that seems to be working out at the moment to the American economy's comparative disadvantage in world competition. More and better-trained and better-educated employees will help. But how much? And would this mean more jobs and less unemployment (which seems plausible), or would it work the other way (as is sometimes claimed)?

It has been argued forcefully elsewhere that as "the provision of services has displaced the production of goods as the country's principal economic activity, . . . human capital, defined as the 'skill, dexterity and knowledge' of the population, has become the critical input that determines the rate of growth of the economy. . . ."* This is backed up by data apparently indicating that "the increase in the number and education of the work force and the greater pool of knowledge available to the workers" have accounted for as much as two-thirds of the increased growth of the economy over the past 30 years or so. This is identified then with an increase in total national expenditures for education from $8.3 billion in 1950 to $141.5 billion in 1979. This seems a powerful dollars-and-cents argument not only for improving the traditional education offering but for extending it to men and women already in the work force.

Yet other economists warn against the arithmetic of "human capital economics," finding it so flawed as to be essentially unreliable. In political terms, a new federal administration, espousing an emphasis on the supply side of economic development—which would appear, logically, to be augmented by increased and improved education—is recommending large reductions in federal education appropriations. Lifelong-learning initiatives in the Congress have received over the years, despite the arguments made for them in economic

---

* Ginzberg and Vojta, The Service Sector of the U. S. Economy, March, 1981, *Scientific American,* p. 48 ff.

terms, exceedingly short shrift. Something is missing in either the theory of human capital economics or its transferability into essential operational terms.

The argument appears plausible, too, that making education into the larger scale growth industry it could become would in itself afford significant stimulus to the economy. But nobody has done what would appear to be the relatively simple analysis that would at least tend to prove or disprove this.

It is suggested that the adoption in this country of the now widespread European practice of granting "educational leaves of absence" to currently employed workers would mean both an up-grading of the workforce and a reduction in the unemployment rate, by the number of replacement workers required. But this evokes little national interest here, and the reports from East Germany and France are that slight use is being made of the leave-of-absence option.

Even modest suggestions about readjusting the unemployment compensation system so as to make it a countercyclical economic measure and to permit laid-off employees to use the idle time for retraining and education attract little notice and less effective support.

It seems a fair assumption that at least part of the reason the architects of this volume seem to shy away from arguing the case for adult education in broad economic system terms is that there is so little firm evidence to go on in making what appears on the face of it so promising. They do, though, recognize this additional line of support for their thesis—even to the point of emphasizing it fairly strongly as they look in their last chapter toward "More Distant Shores." In a sense there is one book written fully and carefully here, and then the outline of another. It seems almost imperative that the other book—An Economy in Transition: The Learning Connection—be written.

If one reason for down-playing the overall economics of adult education is uncertainty about how they actually work out, another involves a proper concern about the narrowing effect of building any major educational initiative around only its economic worth. It would be a great loss if adult education were to become, in this country, only adult vocational education.

A clear consciousness of this is reflected in the chapter here on employer tuition assistance programs. The argument is made strongly that the restriction of such assistance to job-related training courses is a mistake from the standpoint of employees, employers, and the general public as well. There has been significant recognition of this in the Congress' 1978 amendment of the Internal Revenue Act so as to extend the tax deductibility of tuition assistance payments to cover virtually all types of educational courses.

This same set of concerns and interests is expressed in broader form in the inclusion among "worklife transitions" of the passage from, in traditional terms, employment to retirement. Perhaps the making of substantial provision for educational renewal opportunities at this increasingly populated transfer point can be translated into terms of another significant growth potential for the economy as a whole. But this isn't the most obvious purpose or value here. What adult education should be offering life's senior class is a curriculum opening up the widest possible array of opportunities for whatever pursuits are appealing, including perhaps particularly the improved use of leisure.

This question of whether adult education is to be narrowly or broadly oriented, along occupational or widely differentiated lines, may well affect the society's future fundamentally. We recognize the critical importance of this balance in the education prescribed for youth, maintaining a constant constructive tension between the advocacy of general, liberal arts learning on the one hand and vocational training on the other. Although the course and content of adult education will obviously be a matter of free individual choice, it may well be that the society has as large a stake in adults' learning being broad gauge as it has in young people's knowing at least something of the liberal arts.

Perhaps it risks false emphasis to make this point, illustratively, in terms of the current pace of change in the relationship between people and technology. It is this change that has contributed more than any other single factor to the frequency of worklife transitions; and the most obvious or at least immediate importance of the learning connection is in equipping people to meet the impact of this change. Yet these transitions in particular individuals' work lives and their success in accommodating to them are only a small part of what is involved here.

Philosophers have warned for a long time about this development. Thorstein Veblen's prediction was that the free society would find its ultimate testing in whether it could stand the inevitable stresses between the human purpose and what he called scientific invention. He was characteristically gloomy about the prospect. In Karel Capek's classic of the 1920's, Rossum's Universal Robots took over. So did George Orwell's Big Brother.

Alfred North Whitehead considered technology of no less force and significance, but gave "man" at least a chance:

> The greatest invention of the nineteenth century was the invention of the method of invention. A new method entered into life. In order to understand our epoch, we can neglect all the details of change, such as railways, telegraphs, radios, spinning machines, synthetic dyes. We must concentrate on the method itself; that is the real novelty, which has broken up the foundations of the old civilisation. The prophecy of Francis Bacon has now been fulfilled; and man, who at times dreamt of himself as a little lower than the angels, has submitted to become the servant and the minister of nature. It still remains to be seen whether the same actor can play both parts.

It won't be enough to qualify the same actors to both serve and manage "the method of invention" that they learn how to meet, in their own work lives, the competition of some new device or process. There is the at least equal need, in the democratic society, for constantly requalifying the full membership to meet the changing demands on it for societal decision-making.

To recognize when you become one of life's seniors how much wasn't taught you in school because it hadn't happened at the time is to question seriously your capacity or entitlement to even enter into the management of the society's affairs. Even if you "try to keep up," you realize that your children know a great deal more than you do about the fission and fusion of the atom, non-recombinant genes, computers, and the geo-politics of a world whose map bears little resemblance except on two of the continents to the one you learned in school.

It seems gratuitous to develop the case that a continuing educational opportunity is as important to the discharge of citizenship's responsibilities as it is to holding onto a job or being able to move to another one. Paul Barton and company have served us well in refusing to limit their argument for adult education to its immediate cost effectiveness, and in concentrating on the human values in a lifetime learning connection.

* * * *

A brief post-script:

It remains as true as it was before that no worthwhile book or report can be written by a committee. To know a little, though, about how this particular volume was put together and about the degree of participation of virtually all of the twenty-nine members of the National Advisory Committee is to want to qualify the broad generalization. Their role went far beyond advice and consent. Many of the ideas here have a widely mixed parentage. This is a very different book from what any one person would have written alone. If it is right that the advocacy here reflects an extraordinary integrity, this is at least partly because whatever weaker arguments were advanced withered in the heat of their testing within the councils of the committee.

Noting this would be gratuitous if it were only editorial comment. The broader point is that such a process commends itself not only for writing a book about adult education but for implementing the course that is marked out. The institutional identifications of the Committee members don't diminish the larger truth that they are all committed as individuals to what John Gardner has called the private pursuit of the public interest. One of the few small prides of the National Institute for Work and Learning is in its commitment to the idea that part of democracy's strength, so far too little drawn on, lies in the development of an effective collaborative process within the private sector.

WILLARD WIRTZ

Preface

Major advances in provision for continued learning during working life will require close working relationships among employers, educators, unions, and government. Both in the commissioning of this book by the National Institute of Education and in the writing of it by the National Institute for Work and Learning*, it was decided that representatives from these sectors would be involved in its development. The National Advisory Committee on Worker Education and Training Policy has participated at every step, including two meetings at which the outline for it was reviewed, one meeting discussing progress on various commissioned papers that were to provide background for it, two meetings reviewing draft chapters, and correspondence with individual members on chapters as they evolved. Discussion was often vigorous, but at all times constructive; not all members would agree with all statements and recommendations, but there is broad consensus on central purpose and policy directions.

The National Advisory Committee is as follows:

Marla Batchelder, Personnel Solutions, Inc.
Marvin Berkeley, North Texas State University
Joseph Bertotti, University of South Florida
Len Brice, American Society for Personnel Administration
Bruce Carswell, General Telephone and Electronics
John Chadwell, Owens-Illinois
Robert Craig, American Society for Training and Development
Walter Davis, AFL-CIO
Richard Drabant, Chrysler Corporation
Russell Farnen, Empire State College
Murray Frank, University of Massachusetts
Donald Fronzaglia, Polaroid Corporation
Sean Gibney, American Federation of State, County, and Municipal Employees
William Gary, International Union of Electrical, Radio and Machine Workers
Nathaniel Hackney, Hospital and Health Care Employees
James Hall, Empire State College
Reese Hammond, International Union of Operating Engineers
Richard Holan, United States Steel Corporation
Richard Hupp, Kimberly Clark de Mexico, S.A.
Carroll Hutton, United Auto Workers

---

* Formerly, the National Manpower Institute

Robert Jones, General Motors Corporation
John Kulstad, Communication Workers of America
Norman Kurland, New York State Department of Education
Joyce Miller, Amalgamated Clothing and Textile Workers Union
Robert Nielsen, American Federation of Teachers
Kiernan O'Reilly, General Telephone and Electronics
John Stagg, Graphic Arts International Union
Peter Williams, IBM Corporation
Roger Yarrington, American Association of Community and Junior Colleges

I would like to thank the Committee for the time that has been invested in the project, and for the understanding with which the members reviewed first drafts that were often sprinkled with clumsy prose and incomplete thoughts.

The actual researching and writing of the book was an effort in which a number of Institute staff members and consultants were involved. The book itself is part of a larger Institute effort, called the Worker Education and Training Policy Project, directed by Gregory B. Smith, and monitored at the National Institute of Education by Ms. Nevzer Stacy, to which we were responsible for the performance of the contract. Marc Tucker, also of N.I.E., contributed to a significant broadening of the list of policy considerations dealt with in this book. Herbert Levine served as Senior Study Consultant to the project. Gregory Smith directed the preparation of 14 policy research papers by Institute staff members and consultants, papers that provided the underlying knowledge base for many of the chapters, and generally made sure the project stayed on time and on target.

More specifically with regard to staff and consultant contribution, this book owes much to Bryna Shore Fraser, particularly in the area of the structure of existing learning opportunity; to Ivan Charner for the knowledge base on the nature of participation; to Francis Macy with respect to educational counseling for adults; to Charles Stewart who served as a consultant on the use of training programs to assist the unemployed and to assist in economic adjustment generally; to Harold Goldstein, consultant in the area of training in private industry; to Jane Shore for expertise on tuition-aid programs (and also for substantial editing); to Julia French for work on older workers; to Robert Sexton, consultant with regard to equal treatment for part-time students; to Denise Wilder for a complete review of education and training programs from the perspective of women; and to Anne Rogers who took over the editing at mid-point in the writing. Typing and retyping a book is a considerable task, and we thank Sylvia Bruce for it.

The President of the Institute, Archie E. Lapointe, provided the environment and encouragement necessary for a collaborative venture such as this, and Willard Wirtz gave the project its existence, by virtue of his prior work in creating an "education-work" policy, and his dedication to a collaborative approach to problem solving.

As the leader of this team effort I had as much assistance as any author could ever hope for, and any inadequacies in the product are entirely my responsibility.

PAUL E. BARTON

Worklife
Transitions

Chapter 1

The Learning Connection

Is not indeed every man a student?

Ralph Waldo Emerson, 1841

And every woman?

1981

Inadequate productivity, unemployment lines in industries hard hit by imports, women who want to go back to work but are without credentials, immigrants adjusting to a new country, older workers who fear the rocking chair, and blue-collar workers who want to study literature are all situations that have something in common. There is a learning connection to all of them. These learning connections occur in adult life, and take education far beyond its traditional role of preparing youth to enter society.

The notion that education is a *prelude* to life rather than a *part* of life has, until recently, formed the base upon which the public and private education systems were built. But strong forces of change and higher aspirations among the American population are combining to ensure that this notion will no longer dominate educational policy.

There was a time when human societies lived by a relatively unchanging body of knowledge which told individuals and groups how to relate to each other and secure clothing, food, and shelter. In the beginning, the family passed this knowledge on. Much later, the family and the school shared responsibility for passing on accumulated knowledge. But this country has rushed us toward a new state of affairs which demands that we learn in order to live, that we continue to learn throughout every decade of life.

As we enter the 1980s, the nation has accepted a pace of change that means the education and experiences we gain early in life are no longer adequate preparation for our entire lives. We accept accelerating change and the need to adapt, recognizing learning's role in successful adaptation.

From a historical perspective, there is an increasing discontinuity, for any individual at any age, between the past, the present, and the future. The purposes of education during youth, including the socialization of the young into adult society, are less likely to be achieved when the past experiences of that society—experiences of classroom teacher, parent, or grandparent—are so different from the current experience of the young person, particularly when that young person's experience is continually and rapidly changing.

In this sea of change, we are all looking for a beacon to guide us toward safe harbors. Familiar roles and predictable futures provided such assurance in traditional societies and, in this sense, most of us are much less assured than we want and need to be. One as yet dim beacon—the potential for learning throughout life—may promise some assurance that adaptations can be made when needed. The ideas of changing society and unchanging knowledge are quite abstract, but easily visualized in common, real-life situations, such as:

- The advertising account executive left behind by new multimedia techniques;

- The schoolteacher facing new concepts of teaching math;

- The researcher lost among new multiple regression techniques and "dummy variables";

- The factory worker watching new and strange equipment installed;

- The central office manager after a major decentralization of administrative control; and

- The newly minted Ph.D. trying to enter a declining teaching profession that was booming when he or she chose an academic career in high school.

These examples have obvious learning connections. Formal learning opportunities may not help an elderly person dismayed by a modern subway system or an out-of-work miner who doesn't want to pull up stakes in a one-industry town. But for many, a new learning opportunity may be the way to keep pace with social and economic change.

The acceleration of change is not limited to the effect of new machinery and new processes on our lives. Rapid economic and technological change is accompanied by rapidly changing roles in families and in the economy. The changes in family structure and relationships are transforming the lives of more and more people. The transformation is not uniform across the nation, however, for the roles people play in relation to other family members vary tremendously by income and ethnic group and by racial origins. While all Americans are subject to similar pressures and forces, different traditions foretell different reactions to change.

More and more frequently, older people are living alone or in communities for older people. One result is that older people have fewer functions to perform within the family, functions that in the past occupied time and provided purposes. Grandparents were repositories of wisdom and experience to be drawn upon by younger family members; their much-appreciated skills ranged from baking pies to caring for children, and tending gardens to mending toys. These new live-apart arrangements have brought older people increased time and reduced purpose. Leisure is no longer an unskilled occupation.

The disappearance of long-accepted roles for older people is a result of earlier retirements and the growing predominance of the nuclear family. While this has vast implications for millions of people over 65, there is as yet no social response to filling the void in their lives. Senior citizens' clubs and discounts at the theatre box office amount to a few drops of water in a desert. An exploration of the learning connection could make the later years more useful and fulfilling. It is easy to see from our own observations that older people who retain their interest in and enthusiasm about life are also people who continue to learn. Education for them can be a savoring of life, and not just preparation for it.

While the situation of older people within family and society simply festers, women's roles have undergone an explosion of change. The traditional woman's role of caring for a family and a male breadwinner has been changing for decades. But anyone who reads the newspapers, scans the titles in a bookstore, or lives in a family can testify to the especially rapid pace of recent change.

While the public record (as represented by our statistics on employment and the Gross National Product) still considers women's work in the home to have no monetary value, women are leaving the home for the workworld in numbers that for years have exceeded the projections of Bureau of Labor Statistics technicians. Women enter the workworld from the home with four handicaps. The education many received when young did not prepare them to enter today's market. Whatever employment skills they did have deteriorated relative to market demand during the years they were working in the home. And women still face occupational stereotyping in the employment world.

But the most serious problem women face in the workworld is an old and pernicious one—sex discrimination. Often their own aspirations are eroded by messages from society and its agents. But as these obstacles are overcome, there will remain a residue of learning needs to compensate for past neglect by the educational system and years of experience lost while mates were pursuing their own careers.

There is, in these social roles that change the lives of older people and women, a learning connection.

The U.S. economic system requires learning throughout life, not only as a result of changes in the economy (which impels people back to the classroom for retooling), but also because of its vast need for skilled and educated workers and managers (to make the machinery of production run smoothly). Industry has probably never really accepted the prevailing idea among those in public education that formal learning is completed between ages 17 and 21. To the contrary, private industry investment in education and training is very large and probably growing. However, this sector of adult learning is not generally noticed and remains largely unmeasured by statisticians.

The nation has had reason throughout its history to evaluate its learning enterprise from the standpoint of ability to produce. In the 1940s, systematic industrial training became necessary in World War II, due to the conversions of plants for military equipment and the hiring of inexperienced people. The launching of Sputnik made us reexamine the training of mathematicians and scientists in the mid-1950s. As we enter the 1980s, a confluence of events again requires a careful assessment of whether our investments in learning are adequate, from kindergarten through working life.

While inflation in the U.S. has usually been held to the level of a low-grade fever, it is sometimes a rampant infection that proves very difficult to treat. Resistant as inflation is to the economists' black bag of treatments, no one could claim that increased investments in skills training would have an immediate or large effect. Nevertheless, it is prudent to look carefully at industries where shortages of trained people are creating production bottlenecks, or driving up costs as employers bid against each other for the few trained people available. While our national recordkeeping is not generally good enough to spot these bottlenecks, particularly before the situation becomes serious and lead time for training no longer exists, there is consensus that there are now severe shortages in certain areas for technicians, particularly in the computer sciences.

Almost any meeting of corporate trainers and recruiters produces stories about the difficulty of finding people with skills in critical need. Yet there are few relationships established between education and employment institutions to get warning signals sent to the right place at the right time. Nor do the federal government's economic accounts and statistics measure these deficiencies in personnel or the job vacancies that cannot be filled.

The nation's economic ills include what is called a decline in "productivity." Although productivity is measured in terms of output per person hour, this is a convenient measure rather than an indication that changes in productivity result from changes in how fast or how competently workers perform their tasks. Productivity also will decline if management decisions are unwise or plant and equipment are old and inefficient.

Productivity is also as much a matter of the dedication and commitment of both workers and managers, as of management systems and engineering change. It requires the kind of drive that erected and occupied the Empire State Building in 14 months, not the three and a half years it would take today.

For whatever reason—and probably for a combination of reasons—productivity declined seriously during the 1970s, and it shows no signs of improving. This adversely affects unit costs, feeds inflation, and worsens our competitive position in the world economy. Statistical analyses over long periods of time attribute some portion of growth in productivity in the United States to education and training. While these measurements are by no means precise, our economic predicament makes it desirable to review our levels of investment in development of human resources from the standpoint of the efficiency of the economic machinery upon which we all depend. We are handicapped by having almost no solid information, at the plant level, about how changes in training investments affect productivity.

Exploring the learning connection to economic growth and productivity is particularly critical as the nation enters these last two decades of the 20th century. The drying up of oil supplies; the realization that the industrial process upon which we rely pollutes the planet; the careening of the economy between inflation and recession; the decline of the dollar abroad; and the fear that our aging industrial plant has become less productive than those of other countries, have all created more uncertainty about the economic future than at any time since the 1930s. How much does renewed national confidence and capability depend on greater development of human potential and capability? How much can we compensate for constraints in other areas by developing a more highly skilled workforce and better training for corporate managers capable of planning ways around the roadblocks to continued growth? The answer, of course, is that we don't know, and won't until we make the effort to find out.

In the spring of 1981 the debate in Washington was on how to slow inflation and increase productivity. This debate was almost wholly carried on in terms of "supply side" economics vs. Keynesian economics, or the size of budget or tax cuts, or the Federal Reserve's control of growth of the money supply. But the question of whether there is a learning connection to finding new ways to grow or increasing output through investments in human resources is largely ignored.

While new economic imperatives demand a search for new learning connections, old-style, garden-variety economic and market shifts create dislocations in the lives of workers that are all too often shouldered by the individual and the family, rather than by the system as a whole. While these changes are necessary to the system and benefit workers as a whole, they can be traumatic for many individuals; without help in personal readjustment, customary standards of living are difficult to maintain. The kinds of changes that cause serious occupational dislocation, year in and year out, are fairly well known.

The most dramatic kind of change (although not necessarily the most prevalent) results from the introduction of new technology, where a piece of machinery or an industrial process renders the skills of workers using old machinery or processes obsolete. These workers have to be retooled either for the new technology or for jobs in other firms or occupations. Another wrenching change occurs within the declining industry where jobs are reduced inexorably, year by year, sometimes within geographical areas almost entirely dependent on that industry. Change also results when industries gradually relocate, moving from the Northeast to the South, for example. Many workers are being dislocated from their accustomed occupations by increases in imports, although the federal government does provide these workers substantial readjustment assistance. Lastly, hundreds of thousands of workers, idled by periodic recessions, could make productive use of this downtime for education and training to help them adapt to forced occupational change.

The burden of making these adjustments must not fall wholly on the shoulders of individual workers and their families. We have perfected a system of income maintenance, Unemployment Insurance, to cushion the immediate economic loss. But we have taken only limited and halting steps to help those workers who must change occupations and learn the skills necessary to do so. A worker thrown out of a job by increased imports is entitled to retraining assistance, while receiving cash assistance for living expenses. But that is virtually the only condition under which such assistance is made available. If family economic circumstances deteriorate to the point where the poverty or low-income criteria of the Comprehensive Employment and Training Act (CETA) program are met, then there may be assistance if openings in training programs occur. But is it wise public policy to wait until workers and their families fall into poverty before helping them to acquire new skills? The learning connection can figure in cushioning the shock of occupational dislocation.

Changes in the composition of the population, and the rates at which different segments of the population grow, affect both the demand and the need for education and training. As birth control became widely available, couples married later and had fewer children; population growth has leveled off to the point that the 1980s will see an actual decline in the number of teenagers. This may mean an easing of the severe teenage unemployment problem. But it also means two very important things for adult learning. First, investment in youth education will decrease, and hard-pressed public budgets may find it easier to handle the financing of adult learning. More importantly, many resources, from school buildings to instructional personnel, are becoming available which could be converted to the instruction of adults. One qualification, however, is that many school systems, particularly in the inner city, are inadequately funded and staffed; great concern exists about the quality of basic instruction in these systems. So there remains a demand for enlarged youth education budgets, and it should be remembered that minority teenage population growth will not peak until the middle of the decade.

Population growth in the 1980s will be concentrated in the "prime working age" group, those between 25 and 54 years of age, who have the highest labor-force participation rates. The World War II baby boom will occupy roughly the middle of this age spectrum, but will be bolstered at the lower end by the continued high birthrates of the 1950s. The magnitude of growth in this 25- to 54-year-old group (from 1977 to 1990) is quite large—22.8 million out of a net increase of 23.8 million for total labor-force participation, age 16 and over. When changing labor-force participation rates are factored in, the Bureau of Labor Statistics (intermediate projection) expects an increase in the labor force of 24.1 million 25- to 54-year-olds in the same time frame, larger than the total growth of 21.4 million, reflecting a decline in the other sectors of the labor-force age spectrum.

This growth in the middle of the labor-force age span is good news for the economy, for it means a large supply of the most experienced and productive members of the population. But it also means increasing competition for diminishing advancement opportunities within pyramid-structured organizations. This will be the most highly educated group of middle-aged adults this society has ever seen and a group probably with the highest aspirations. What needs to be explored is whether new interrelationships between work and learning can help meet these aspirations, by promoting horizontal mobility among a variety of jobs, as well as upward mobility within occupational fields. One other significant fact is that those who have the most education when young most frequently return to it when older. Therefore, we can expect this growth in the labor force to be reflected in the adult education and training statistics as well.

This growth spurt in the 25- to 54-year-old labor force during the 1980s is not entirely due to population growth. Another important cause is that more women will be working. As we entered the decade of the 1950s, slightly more than one-third of all women 16 and over were in the labor force. By the mid-1960s, it was two out of five. The labor-force entry rate accelerated until, by 1978, it was exactly one out of every two and rising. By June 1980, the labor-force participation rate for women 16 and over stood at 52 percent, with the U.S. Bureau of Labor Statistics (BLS) projecting it would rise to 57 percent (intermediate growth estimate) or 60.4 percent (high growth estimate) by 1990. For a long time, the rate of women's entry into the labor force has been more rapid than officially projected, so these new BLS figures may underestimate the decade's potential growth.

The prospect of women pouring into the labor force has important implications for worklife learning. The first is that many women have been out of the labor force for a long time and they will need some form of education or training to make the transition. The second is that since we are far from achieving occupational parity between men and women, catching up will require enlarging access to learning for women who work. Unfortunately, it is more complicated than simply adding time in the classroom, for many working women already have two jobs, meeting the demands of an employer and meeting the demands of a household. This double burden has to be reckoned with in any effort to enlarge learning opportunity.

Complicating labor-force adjustments in 1980 is the situation of older workers and changing attitudes toward retirement. The modern industrial society made it possible for the older person to give up back-breaking physical work. But as work became physically easier, people continued to retire at even earlier ages, either voluntarily—enticed by liberal retirement benefits—or forced out by mandatory retirement policies. By 1970, the years of life *not* spent in work averaged 27 years for men and 51 years for women, a result of longer education before full-time work, longer lives, and earlier retirement. Today older workers find that inflation makes it harder to live on a fixed income, mandatory retirement is outlawed before age 70, the social security program is short on revenue and long on expenditures, and the proportion of older people in the population is rising.

Coupled with retirement laws and inflation, the demography of the situation will prompt a new look at retirement policies in the 1980s. From 1950 to 1980, the population aged 25 to 64 grew by 40 percent, while the population aged 65 and over almost exactly doubled. The growth of the 65-and-over group will continue into the 1980s, then dip in the 1990s until the World War II baby boom explodes the population of the traditional retirement-age group beginning in the first decade of the next century. Important choices are involved, stemming from the probability that more people are going to be working longer; closer links between work and education will be required as older persons prepare for second and third careers, and employers will probably seek to update the skills of many workers who in other times were either encouraged or forced to retire.

The fact that the United States embraces both opportunity for all and equality among individuals and groups does not mean that the pursuit of one guarantees the achievement of the other. Equal opportunity offered to people with unequal abilities, caused by barriers to their education or past lack of opportunity, will not necessarily lead to equality, although it is a necessary precondition. Nor does a policy of equality in access to opportunity in itself enlarge those opportunities. When we enlarge opportunity for learning during working life, we must also plan to create more equal access to it.

Those who have had the least education when young frequently take least advantage of learning opportunities when older. A close look at this pattern reveals that its origins are not at all mysterious. One reason for lower participation among adults with less formal schooling is that those who left school early often had the worst experience with education and retain this feeling when older. The other reason, though, is that groups with the least education are more likely to face barriers to returning. If we enlarge opportunity for learning without lowering these barriers, we will widen the learning gaps between different segments of the population rather than contribute to their narrowing. But if we simultaneously attend to these barriers, enlarged opportunity may become synonymous with increased equality.

The barriers of which we speak often are not difficult to remove; what they require is acknowledgment and careful attention. So simple a matter as providing good information about community learning opportunities to those outside existing networks would help substantially. A study of tuition-aid plans revealed that half the workers did not even know that their employer offered a plan or that it paid tuition for school. Other workers not now participating in education need counseling for help with application procedures. Others want courses offered at less threatening places, such as the workplace or union hall. Others do not know that many colleges and universities give academic credit for those life and work experiences with college-level educational content.

Some of these barriers are more difficult to deal with than others. Working women may need additional education and training to gain access to the kinds of jobs men have, but they are already doubly burdened by working at a job and caring for a family. (Recent surveys show that while there is much talk of men sharing in housework, few husbands actually help with the household chores.) The time and energy simply are not there. Approaches to this situation include more part-time employment opportunities, more flexible working hours, and better arrangements for child care.

Another important question is whether greater learning opportunities can contribute to greater equality of economic opportunity. For example, while the percentages of youth getting high school diplomas are nearly equal among whites and blacks, this equality has arrived too late to benefit the 50-year-old black. Expanded adult education opportunities may help, although we know little about the degree to which educational gains can be translated into economic gains among older groups.

In the case of women, readjusting the patterns of occupational access will require a companion effort to enlarge opportunities for education and training in the adult years. While there are efforts to open occupational preparation programs equally to women and men, these efforts may be too late for the woman of 35 wanting to return to the labor force but lacking the skills to compete for jobs in occupations traditionally reserved for men.

Throughout the nation's history, new waves of immigrants have brought new traditions, energy, and hope to the society and its economy. This is no less true for the current wave of immigrants. While the public school systems once again bear the major burden of integrating the children of immigrants into American society, adults cannot be excluded. For many years, adult education in the United States was almost synonymous with Americanization classes for citizenship, a tradition we need to revive in a modernized form.

Learning opportunity is essential on two fronts. First, skill training is needed for those who left their countries without the occupational training to make it in the United States. To a considerable extent, this is the approach being used with Vietnamese refugees. If a general training adjustment program existed, like the special programs for workers unemployed from the effects of foreign trade, it could be used here. The CETA program will provide limited training, but these funds are increasingly directed only to people with very low incomes. Secondly, the language problem is more complex than it was in the past. It must be handled with a sensitivity that recognizes the need both to function in an English-speaking society and to retain identities and traditions derived from other cultures.

This is not to suggest that only immigrants have problems functioning in an English-speaking society. Millions of adult Americans do not read well enough to function adequately in an economy that demands a literate work-force. Progress is, to be sure, considerable as more and more adults each decade have at least eight years of schooling. But in a test given in 1974 to a national sample of 26- to 35-year-olds (who are much better educated than any older group), one out of five, after reading a sign that said "Horsepower Without Horse Sense Is Fatal," could not correctly choose among a highway, a gymnasium floor, a racetrack, or a grocery store the place where "you would probably see this sign."

It should not be assumed that all economic and social changes with a potential learning connection are grim changes. Learning during what was once wholly a working period of life represents a new opportunity precipitated by the tremendous success of the American system of government and economy. Learning is more attainable because this society has one of the highest per capita incomes of any nation in history. More people can combine work with education because a higher proportion than ever before of those 20 to 55 years old are in the paid labor force, earning the money to pay for learning, as well as being exposed to learning at the workplace.

Education and training are ever more accessible to adults because prior generations have ensured that time and money will be available. To be sure, barriers to universal availability remain, but this fact should not obscure the major advances made and the opportunities in place for tens of millions of adults, many of them working:

- Tuition-aid programs as a regular employment benefit for blue-collar workers.

- Community colleges with thick catalogues of adult offerings and very low tuition.

- Families with the means to pursue education simply for enjoyment—literature, art, music, Civil War history—rather than out of occupational necessity.

- A history class, or a physics class, on the 6:30 A.M. educational television channel.

- Opportunities for women to leave the home to receive education and training for jobs that will add purpose as well as income to their lives.

To make learning a part of life rather than a preparation for it, a means of finding greater purpose and fulfillment rather than a response to grim necessity, are objectives well worth the effort. Adaptation to social and economic change triggers a learning connection. But learning also promises greater personal and societal fulfillment and purpose. These twin connections, while distinct, are closely related: both make learning a significant part of a whole life.

* * * *

We have sought to describe learning opportunities wherever they are or could be, whether in public schools, in vocational or technical schools, on the factory floor, in community colleges or universities, in union halls, on the television, at the YWCA, through the mail, or from the county agent.

We are interested not only in educational opportunities, but also in equal access to them, and in the quality of the opportunity as well as the quantity. And we seek to learn how our institutions can work together to make the learning connection.

Chapter 2

The Outline
of Opportunity

The most recent . . . survey . . . puts the total figure for adults 17 and older who are involved in further education or training on a part-time basis at . . . 11.6 percent of the eligible population.

> Michael O'Keefe, *The Adult, Education, and Public Policy*, 1976

Although the degree of participation varies, almost every adult appears to undertake at least some learning activities every year.

> Patrick R. Penland, *Self-Planned Learning in America*, 1977

The short of it is that there is simply no comprehensive or integrated set of work training measurements in the United States.

> Willard Wirtz and Harold Goldstein, *A Critical Look at the Measuring of Work*, 1975

All three of the above commentators on adult education and training in the United States were writing within a three-year time span. Each report quite accurately describes a truth derived from available measurements about the state of learning among adults. When we ask about the size of the education and training effort of young people, the response will be primarily based on a single, widely used measure—attendance taken daily in the public classroom. This is not at all the case, however, for adult learning during the working period of life.

The most official measure of adult education, the National Center for Education Statistics (NCES) figures used by Michael O'Keefe, are based on part-time attendance in organized instruction among persons 17 years of age and over. By this measure, participation has increased from 7.6 percent of the population in 1957 to 11.6 percent in 1975.[1] Patrick Penland's optimistic report that practically all adults have a learning activity during the course of a year is based on private surveys of learning that include self-planned and self-directed learning. This learning is frequently undertaken to satisfy curiosity or to fill a specific need for information, as, for example, studying a foreign language prior to traveling abroad. Estimates of the magnitude of such learning range from 79 percent to 98 percent of the adult population.[2] Other estimates of adult education activity fall between 11.6 percent and 98 percent participation, depending on the definition used.

The NCES data are limited in several respects. Only school-based instruction is measured. Only individuals over the compulsory school age of 16 are counted, although our popular definition of youth extends to age 18 or 21. Furthermore, restricting adult education to part-time attendance ignores the worker who goes to school full-time on an education sabbatical and the housewife who returns to school full-time before going back to work. Moreover, the data measure *education* rather than *learning* in a broad sense.

A number of people have struggled with the problem of definitions. What is education and what is training? What is the difference between the terms "education" and "learning"? Should learning in adult worklife be called simply "adult education"? "continuing education"? "recurrent education"? "lifelong learning"? And can education for worklife be neatly separated from education pursued for other purposes? In attempting to find a useful means of classification, the NCES makes a distinction between nonorganized and organized instruction, clearly implying that only the latter is subject to measurement. This ignores informal on-the-job training as well as carefully planned and executed self-learning projects, by equating learning with the classroom.

A more inclusive means of classification, developed by an Educational Testing Service (ETS) team of researchers, uses a category of "deliberate learning" to include education offered by schools, nonschool organizations, and individually used sources.[3] The ETS classification provides for a second category, "unintentional learning," which takes place in the home or at work and is gained from friends, the mass media, and daily experience, although we believe that much of this learning is more intentional than this label suggests.[4] The ETS classification of deliberate learning is the most comprehensive we have seen, and it constitutes the starting point for work on this chapter's outline of opportunity.

It best serves the purposes of this volume to summarize all known "organized learning" activity in which adults engage wherever it takes place. This excludes learning that takes place through newspapers, magazines, television, etc., which has never been measured. Nor does "organized learning" include what we learn from daily life experience, although we are mindful of the wisdom in Alexis de Tocqueville's observation that "true information is mainly derived from experience."[5] And while we choose the term "learning" instead of "education," because education has come to be closely identified with formal schooling, we recognize that the distinction would have been lost on Henry Adams, for whom all learning was education, including his first memory: "He first found himself sitting on a yellow floor in strong sunlight. He was three years old when he took this earliest step in education; a lesson in color."[6]

Having settled on the term "organized learning," we must distinguish between education for youth and for adults during working life, for working life starts at different ages, and youth education ends at different ages—from age 16 for a high school dropout to the late 20s for a doctor. What seems relevant is the *resumption* of education after a substantial interval. Therefore, our definition includes the 20-year-old correspondence school student who dropped out of high school at age 16, but excludes the 21-year-old about to graduate from a four-year college.

This chapter outlines all organized learning for people who have terminated their education in or after high school, or in or after college. Such learning parallels that which occurs during working life, and gives this volume its name of *Worklife Transitions.* Unfortunately, the collectors of the available statistics and estimates have not used our definition, and so the numbers to follow are approximate. Where there are competing estimates and studies, we have included them all. Therefore, our count of organized learning activity ranges from 37,660,000 to 83,615,000 participants, depending on whose estimates are used for any particular component.

PS 10 and Hometown High

Adult Education in Elementary and Secondary Schools

	Participants
Adult Basic Education	660,000
All Other (including GED)	966,000

Although public schools are mostly for the young, many adults still find the education they need there. Adult education programs, offered in most school districts throughout the United States, are aimed primarily at adults who did not complete secondary school but who wish to earn a high school diploma. Usually, the course of study prepares students to take the General Education Development (GED) tests. In 1977, 517,847 persons took the GED exams, and

361,124 of them passed. Sixty percent of those who took the tests were 20 years or older, with the average age 25. Almost 40 percent of the candidates indicated that they were taking the exams in order to gain entrance to additional education or training programs.[7]

Adult Basic Education (ABE) courses, designed to eliminate functional illiteracy, focus mainly on those with less than a fourth-grade education and serve about one-third of adult education participants in elementary and secondary schools. Other programs offer English as a second language and occupational courses, seldom for credit. ABE courses, funded by the federal government through the states under the Adult Education Act of 1966, were allotted $100 million in FY 1979. Most programs receive local and state revenues ($3 million in 1976) in addition to the federal ABE allocations. Most courses are available at no or low cost during the evening at local schools.

What are the educational or economic benefits of these programs for students? According to the 1979 edition of *The Condition of Education,* "Through adult basic and secondary education programs (in FY 1976), 118,071 participants received an eighth-grade diploma, 128,886 entered high school, and 114,222 enrolled in other education." In addition, 18,983 persons were removed from public assistance, 61,610 found jobs, and 44,502 found better employment.[8] This record is particularly impressive considering that the adults who participate in adult education courses in public schools are those most in need of educational assistance to obtain the minimal credentials necessary for entering the labor market.

Postsecondary Education Institutions

Adult Participants in Private and Public Postsecondary Institutions
(survey of individuals)

Sponsor	Participants (1975)
A. Vocational, Trade or Business	1,469,000
Public	814,000
Private	628,000
B. Two-Year Community College type (including junior & vocational institutes)	3,020,000
Public	2,790,000
Private	196,000

C. Four-Year College/	
University	3,257,000
Public	2,358,000
Private	904,000

Source: National Center for Educational Statistics, Wash., D.C., 1978.

A. *Vocational, Trade, Business, and Flight Schools (Noncollegiate Postsecondary)*

Noncollegiate Postsecondary Schools with Occupational Programs

	Enrollment	
Occupation	*Public*	*Private*
Agribusiness	4,220	1,738
Marketing/Distribution	13,573	168,355
Health	55,565	91,203
Home economics	6,406	1,182
Business/Office	77,671	189,576
Technical	22,812	88,533
Trades and industry	170,141	279,353
Total	350,388	819,940

Source: NCES, *The Condition of Education,* 1978, p. 102.

Estimates of noncollegiate postsecondary school enrollment vary, depending on the source, from 1.2 million to 3.1 million for the years 1975 to 1978. These discrepancies underscore how the lack of standardized measurement obscures our understanding of adult participation in postsecondary education.[9]

Adults generally enroll in noncollegiate postsecondary schools for one of two reasons: to gain employment or career skills in order to secure a new job or move ahead in the present one, or to pursue a personal avocation, such as dance, music, or karate. Evidence regarding the effectiveness of private or public schools in serving student career needs is mixed. Wellford Wilms (1974) found that only two out of ten graduates of professional or technical training programs ever got the jobs for which they had prepared. Eight out of ten graduates from lower-level clerical or service programs got jobs in their fields but, except for secretaries, barely earned even the federal minimum wage. Wilms also found that public and private school graduates had about the same occupational success or, more accurately, lack of it. He concludes that "post-secondary occupational education, both public and private, maintains class and income inequalities rather than overcomes them."[10]

On the other hand, George Nolfi (1977) asserts that the curriculum and quality of instruction offered by the private noncollegiate schools are comparable to those in degree-granting institutions, that their graduates do as well, and that the private schools have higher completion rates. This is particularly significant, according to Nolfi, "for it has been shown that proprietary schools tend to attract students from a somewhat lower strata [*sic*] in socioeconomic and verbal ability terms than do the public vocational schools and community colleges."[11]

According to Otto Koester, both public and private noncollegiate schools will expand in the 1980s into emerging occupational fields such as data processing, administration, and human services, and continue to grow in the areas of allied health, office occupations, cosmetology, and barbering.[12]

B. Two-Year Colleges and Vocational/Technical Institutes

For the adult wishing to resume education, the two-year, degree-granting college is one of the brightest stars to appear on the horizon in recent decades. Enrollments of adult education participants in these institutions have increased from 11.9 percent of all participants in 1969 to 16.4 percent in 1975, as working adults are attracted by flexible schedules, accessible locations, and diverse curricula.[13] In 1979, part-time enrollments reached 2.7 million, up .4 million since 1976.

Two-year postsecondary institutions generally fall into one of four categories, representing varied institutional arrangements and educational philosophies: junior college, a two-year institution offering a program acceptable toward the B.A. degree, a liberal arts program for those not interested in pursuing a B.A., and occupational/career training; branch campus, a two-year institution directly affiliated with a state university offering a program acceptable toward the B.A.; technical institute, a two-year institution requiring a high school diploma or equivalent for admission and emphasizing occupational programs; and vocational-technical center, a school offering occupational programs almost exclusively and not requiring a high school diploma for entrance. (Many two-year colleges are dropping the diploma requirement.) Whether an adult seeks occupational skills, liberal arts courses, or preparation for transferring to a four-year school, the option is available at a two-year school. Enrollments in occupational programs currently surpass those in transfer programs.[14]

The full-time population of these institutions is predominantly young. Of the

195 schools in the sample surveyed by Godfrey and Holmstrom, nearly half reported that 70 percent or more of their full-time students were under 20 years of age, although almost 75 percent reported some full-time students 40 years or older. Part-time students were generally older: 60 percent at branch campuses, 75 percent at junior colleges, and 95 percent at technical institutes were 20 years or older.[15]

Another significant finding was that almost 75 percent of the male students and over 50 percent of the female students were employed. Not only were there high rates of full-time employment among part-time students (85.1 percent for males and 48 percent for females), but the average work week for full-time male students was 26 hours and for female students, 20 hours.

Because most two-year schools are publicly supported, tuition and fees are generally low. Because of their liberal admissions policies, they may attract those would-be learners who have not fared well within the traditional formal education system. These factors may help explain the phenomenal growth which occurred between 1967 and 1977, when the public two-year institutions nearly doubled their share of total enrollments at institutions of higher education to reach 3,913,000 students in 1977, or 34.3 percent of the total.[16]

C. Four-Year Colleges and Universities

Four-year colleges and universities still conjure up images of youth, football games, and fraternities and sororities, beginning immediately after high school and ending exactly four years later. Such images are increasingly at odds with reality. It is instructive to remember that the adult on the campus is not a new phenomenon. Fred Harvey Harrington pointed out in 1977 that

> adult education at the college level began at least a century and a half ago when older students turned up on American campuses as regular degree candidates. It was not uncommon for young men—and young women a little later—to interrupt their schooling in order to earn money before going on to higher education.[17]

Although until recently the trend was toward a younger student population, now a shift in age distribution among college students is evidenced by Bureau of the Census data. The data show that between 1972 and 1976, the percentage of enrolled students under 25 years of age decreased and the percentage of older age groups increased (see Chart 1). Enrollments of students aged 25 and over nearly doubled, a 44.6 percent increase. This may be partly attributed to the many women 35 and over enrolling in college; their number rose from 418,000 in 1972 to 700,000 in 1976, an increase of 67.5 percent.

THE AGE STRUCTURE OF COLLEGE ENROLLMENT
1972 – 1976

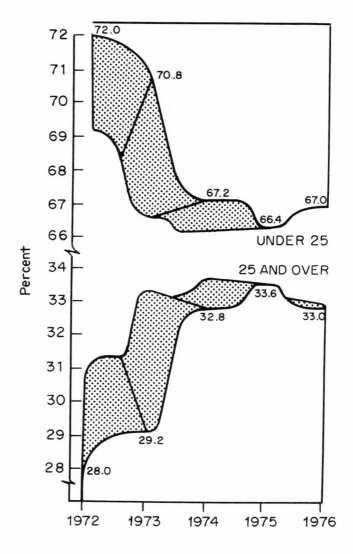

Source: *The Digest of Education Statistics*
1977 - 78, p. 91.

According to the 1975 NCES adult education survey, four-year colleges and universities led in adult education enrollments among postsecondary education institutions. More than 19 percent of adults participating in adult education (3,257,000 individuals) are enrolled in four-year colleges, although the proportion has been declining, probably because two-year colleges and community organizations are offering adult-oriented courses.

Colleges and universities traditionally have provided for the education of adults through their continuing education and extension departments. Approximately 1,230 four-year institutions of higher education operate such programs.[18] Courses are varied, but seldom carry degree credit. Participants are usually well educated and well off. Student fees, which generally support these programs, vary considerably between public and private institutions, credit and noncredit courses.

The number of four-year institutions with extension/continuing education programs has more than doubled since 1967–68, while noncredit participation declined nationally.[19] The increase in extension/continuing education programs reflects institutional efforts to attract a new clientele to offset declining undergraduate enrollments. Colleges and universities are providing more learning opportunities for adults through two separate approaches: adapting

Private Industry and Business

Classroom Education and Training in Large Firms (500 or more employees)

Type	Participants
Company courses	4.4 million
During hours	(3.7) million
After hours	(.7) million
Tuition-aid programs	1.3 million
Other outside courses	.6 million
	6.3 million

Source: Lusterman, 1977

Classroom and Structured On-the-Job Training in Three Industries

Size of Firm	Percentage of Companies Providing Training by
50 to 249 workers	32
250 to 999 workers	44
1,000 workers and over	71

Source: BLS, 1970. Industries are metalworking, electric power, and telephone communications

the delivery of traditional programs to accommodate a nontraditional student population, and offering nontraditional programs to both traditional and non-traditional students. Chapter 8 will take a closer look at the higher education scene.

The two tables above reflect most of what we have learned during the decade of the 1970s about the extent of education and training in private industry. Individual firms keep some information about expenditures for formal class-room training, but little about training done on the job. In fact, most surveys of private industry training have been confined to formal classroom training to the exclusion of that performed on the job. This was true of the survey of large firms published by the Conference Board in 1977 which recorded only those expenditures for education and training incurred directly and did not include wages and salaries paid to employees during training.[20]

On-the-job training has been thought too difficult to measure, particularly since much of it is informal and merges with learning a job through experience. But since this is how a large proportion of workers learn their jobs, the Bureau of Labor Statistics undertook a study to find out if such measurement was feasible and concluded that it was. The above table on three industries gives the results of that study and includes what BLS defined as "structured" on-the-job training.[21]

In view of the limited information available, it is not surprising that esti-mates on total industry expenditures for education and training vary widely.

Government Employers

Estimate of Public Sector Learners

	Number of Learners
Federal civilian employees	515,000
Armed Forces	
Military training	1,590,000
Voluntary Education Program	575,000
U.S. Postal Service	37,500 to 75,000
Tennessee Valley Authority	2,700 to 5,400
State and local governments	731,000 to 1,463,800
Total (approximate)	3.4 to 4.2 million

Source: Composite of estimates by Smith, 1979 and Peterson et al., 1978

The Conference Board study came to an estimate of $2 billion in direct expenditures; another estimate is $100 billion. The middle range of estimates includes $10 billion by Harold Goldstein (private industry only), and $30 to $40 billion (including government) by the American Society for Training and Development.[22] What is known about training and education in private industry is explored in depth in Chapter 6.

According to a study of training in the public sector, there are approximately 19 million employees at the federal, state, and local levels, including uniformed members of the Coast Guard and the four military branches in the Department of Defense. The study estimates that "between three and four million persons receive government-paid and/or sponsored training and education annually" (see table above). The total cost of this education and training activity is nine to ten billion dollars annually.[23]

The Office of Personnel Management (formerly the U.S. Civil Service Commission) and the Department of Defense (DOD) maintain extensive data on training and education for federal civilian and military employees, respectively. Comparatively little is known about other federal employees (e.g., U.S. Postal Service, Tennessee Valley Authority, and the Coast Guard) and the 12,000,000 people employed by state and local governments.

According to 1977 data, 39 percent of federal civilian education and training is dedicated to upgrading employees' technical skills, the remainder to instruction in administration and analysis, legal and scientific topics, supervisory principles, government orientation, clerical skills, trades or crafts, and basic literacy skills.[24] Instruction averages 41 hours and is most usually offered in-house. Opportunities provided outside the government are 77 percent standard academic courses. Blue-collar employees receive only 8.7 percent of the education/training provided, although they represent 24 percent of the population. It was also found that those with the higher salaries had proportionally more education/training experiences, a pattern which lends credence to the belief that those with the least education are least likely to obtain further education or training!

In contrast, the purpose of military training is to prepare personnel to assume jobs in military units. Over 33 percent of all DOD military training is designed to provide initial orientation and indoctrination, over 55 percent is specialized skill training, and over 95 percent provides new skills to participants. DOD offers over 7,000 different courses, ranging in length from five to twenty-five weeks. An average of 214,000 people daily are in formal training, with many attending more than one course annually. In addition to military training, approximately 575,000 service people participate in the Voluntary Education Program as part-time students during their free time at 1,000 cooperating colleges and universities, with 75 percent of tuition costs reimbursed by the military. Each branch also offers high school equivalency programs; in 1975, 80,000 servicemen and women received diplomas.

Also open to learners in all four branches of the military are three major programs. The Defense Activity for Non-Traditional Education Support (DANTES) administers several credit-by-examination programs, including CLEP, ACT, SAT, and overseas GED, and arranges for correspondence courses from civilian schools. The Serviceman's Opportunity College (SOC) is a network of some 360 two-year and four-year postsecondary institutions that offer flexible residency and transfer policies to service personnel. The American Council on Education publishes the *Guide to the Evaluation of Educational Experiences in the Armed Services,* the standard reference work for awarding credit for learning obtained in the military.[25]

No aggregate data are available on training and education for state and local employees, although estimates have been made based on the federal training rate. Several studies point to California as the only state that conducts an annual survey in order to prepare a training report to the Governor.[26] According-ing to a national survey conducted in 1975, two-thirds of all cities with populations greater than 10,000 operate training/education programs. The International City Management Association's study also concluded that among these programs, 90 percent provide on-the-job and specific skill development; 70 percent, supervisory training; 40 percent, interpersonal relations; and 31 percent, team-building. Seventy-three percent engage a college or university to provide the program, although state agencies, private consultants, and professional associations are also major providers.[27]

Federal Employment and Training Programs

New Enrollees in Federal Programs

	New Enrollees
On-the-job training	240,000
Institutional training	2,082,000
Vocational rehabilitation	412,000
Work experience	1,849,000
Public service employment	727,000
	5,310,000

Source: U.S. Budget, Special Analysis, 1978

The federal government's employment and training programs, targeted on the disadvantaged and unemployed, provide skill training for nonprofessional jobs.[28] Of seven major program categories, five concern us here: on-the-job training, institutional training, vocational rehabilitation, work experience, and public service employment. *On-the-job training* programs sponsor training for regular job openings by reimbursing employers who hire disadvantaged persons and retain them after the period of reimbursement. *Institutional training* programs provide vocational skill and job-related remedial education in a classroom setting. *Vocational rehabilitation* programs offer skill training, counseling, allowances, and support services to overcome physical and mental handicaps to employment. *Work experience* provides temporary employment, usually part-time, primarily for young and older workers. *Public service employment* provides transitional public sector jobs to inculcate the work habits and skills needed to compete for regular jobs. These programs are administered by different federal agencies and authorized by different laws, including the Comprehensive Employment and Training Act (CETA), the Work Incentive Program (WIN), the Veterans Rehabilitation Act, and the Vocational Rehabilitation Act.

Federal programs such as CETA and WIN, offering several assistance categories, are shown on a consolidated basis in the U.S. Budget which, unfortunately, does not separate the various categories, and combines the data for youth with that for adults. Nonetheless, the figures provide a rough idea of federally sponsored education and training program participation.

In addition to the federal programs cited above, the Trade Act of 1974 entitles workers "adversely affected" by increased imports to adjustment assistance benefits, including training and related services. According to Department of Labor estimates, of 366,000 eligible workers, approximately 17,000 entered training between 1975 and 1978, and almost 14,000 completed it.[29]

Public retraining programs for unemployed workers are discussed in depth in Chapter 5. As this book goes to press, large budget reductions in CETA activities are being considered by Congress.

Cooperative Extension Service Programs

Extension Activities (1975)

- Extension agent contacts in agriculture and natural resources: 21.6 million
- Home economics: 4,000 agents, 7,000 paraprofessionals and 7,000 volunteers assisted 10 million families
- Community resource development: Extension Service assisted 51,000 community projects.

Source: Extension Service, USDA, June 1976[30]

The State Cooperative Extension Services, through state land-grant universities, work cooperatively with the Extension Service of the U.S. Department of Agriculture to provide educational services under four program categories: agriculture and natural resources, home economics, 4-H youth, and community resource development. Each is designed to involve local people actively, to reflect local priorities and needs. Extension Service agents use intensive individual and group contact methods, supported by mass media approaches. In FY 1976, the federal outlay for extension work totaled almost $229 million, matched by state and county extension funds of almost $298 million. It is almost impossible to estimate the number of individuals reached through the Extension Service yearly, but 11 to 14 million is an approximation.

Agents conducting adult extension programs in agriculture and natural resources made 21.6 million contacts with farmers in 1975. (Each contact does not represent a different individual.) Over 3,000 agricultural agents and more than 3,000 specialists and area staff members devoted 760,000 staff days as follows: 70 percent to commercial farmers; 25 percent to small and low-income farmers; and 5 percent to home gardeners. The agriculture and natural resources program includes crop and livestock production, business management, marketing, and environmental/natural resources.

Through the home economics program, approximately 4,000 Extension Service home economists, 7,000 paraprofessionals, and 700,000 volunteers assist 10 million families annually to "identify their needs, make decisions, and utilize resources to improve their quality of home and family living." Areas of assistance include food and nutrition, family resource management, family life education, family health and safety, and textiles and clothing.

As part of community resource development, the Extension Service in 1975 provided assistance to almost 51,000 community projects, conducted over 9,000 surveys and studies, and led about 55,000 workshops and conferences, reaching some two million people. The program is designed to help communities of 50,000 or fewer make "sound community decisions that will increase economic opportunities and the quality of life in rural areas." Extension Service people work with local government officials to analyze community needs and to promote human services, leadership skills, citizen participation, and governmental effectiveness.

Professional Associations

Professional Society Offerings, 1976

Courses	1,100
Participants	30,000

Source: Greenwald, 1977

Unfortunately for our purposes, the 1975 NCES survey of adult education did not distinguish between professional associations and labor organizations. Therefore, the figure of 1,035,000 participants in courses sponsored by "labor organization or professional association" put forth in the NCES survey does not allow for further analysis.

Professional associations are composed of member practitioners within a particular occupational group and are aimed at advancing the interests of the occupation as a whole as well as enhancing the occupational competence of individual members. These associations are organized on a national, regional, state, or local basis and consist of such diverse memberships as engineers, real estate brokers, doctors, secretaries, and sociologists.

No comprehensive survey of the education and training opportunities offered by these associations exists, although a few associations have carried out their own surveys. In 1977, for example, The American Society of Mechanical Engineers conducted "a comprehensive survey involving a large majority of the major engineering societies." Of the respondents, 86 percent indicated continuing education programs were in operational, developmental, or planning stages.[31]

Another major provider of education to its membership is the combined American Management Association. Its educational resources include 792 staff members, 7,500 lecturers and discussion leaders, 2,000 "formal educational programs," and a budget of $31.8 million.[32]

Clearly, it would be useful to learn more about the educational opportunities offered by professional societies to their members as well as to nonmembers, particularly if it is true that "the professional society, utilizing its vast resources of membership, education, technology, knowledge, and standards, can be a catalyst in the development of new programs that will meet the challenges of technical obsolescence.[33]

Labor Organizations

	Participants
Registered apprentices	300,000
Unregistered apprentices	200,000
Union education department courses	75,000
Labor studies $\}$	offered by 47 higher education institutions
Negotiated tuition aid	in 198 major collective bargaining
	agreements

Source: See Chapter 7.

According to the Department of Labor, there are 224 national and international unions in the United States, including professional and state associations categorized as trade unions, which represent approximately 20 million workers. Peterson et al. estimate that approximately 600,000 union members, or 3 percent of the total, are involved in education and training through four major types of programs: apprenticeship, union education, labor studies, and negotiated tuition-aid plans.

Approximately 500,000 persons are enrolled as apprentices in jointly operated labor-management programs. Almost 300,000 of these are registered with the Bureau of Apprenticeship and Training in the Department of Labor and receive federal funding.[34] It is also estimated that there are perhaps 200,000 unregistered apprentices in the U.S.[35]

Approximately 75,000 union members participate in courses and institutes made available by union education departments, independent of any school or other outside institution. Most of these offerings are "tool" courses, such as shop steward training, leadership training, and contract analysis, designed to improve understanding of unionism and to help union members in their duties as shop stewards and union administrators.

There are two types of labor studies programs: those offered through a university or college and those run by the unions themselves. According to Gray, there are forty-seven institutions of higher education that offer a major or concentration in labor studies, as well as numerous part-time degree programs developed with unions.[36] Unions are engaging in more cooperative ventures with community colleges. A 1977 survey of more than 400 community colleges indicated that 41 percent had developed programs at the request of unions, including apprenticeship training, retraining and upgrading, and labor studies.[37]

Labor studies centers run by unions also offer both degree and "tool" courses to their membership. Degree programs, made possible through affiliations with accredited institutions of higher education, are either in labor studies or liberal arts, with particular emphasis on labor-related issues. Tuition is generally free, as all the union-operated labor studies centers are either sponsored or supported by union funds to offer programs designed exclusively for their members. Well-known centers include the Walter and Mae Reuther Family Education Center, which offers education and training programs independently of any institution of higher education; the George Meany AFL-CIO Labor Studies Center, which offers, in cooperation with Antioch College, an external degree program; and the College of New Rochelle/District Council 37 of the American Federation of State, County, and Municipal Employees (AFSCME), which "represents the first accredited four-year degree program on union premises in the history of America."[38]

According to the most recent data available, about 1.6 million workers are covered under 198 negotiated tuition-aid plans in the United States.[39] Tuition aid is analyzed in detail in Chapter 10. The union involvement in education and training programs is explored at length in Chapter 7.

Community Organizations

Participants in Education Programs, 1972

Churches	3,614,000
Other religions	474,000
Y's & Red Cross	3,050,000
Civic groups	1,175,000
Social service groups	2,285,000
Cultural & other groups	370,000
	10,968,000

Source: NCES, 1972

In 1972, the NCES conducted an extensive survey of adult education offered by community organizations such as churches, other religions, Y's, the Red Cross, civic, social service, cultural, and other groups. About 66,770 (or 28.5 percent) sponsored formal programs of adult instruction serving almost 11 million participants. This figure contrasts markedly with NCES 1972 and 1975 adult education surveys, which reported figures of 1,996,000 and 1,784,000, respectively. In an effort to explain this 9-million-person discrepancy, those reporting the higher figure stated that "although this disparity of nine million is large, a number of factors may help explain the difference. These factors include coverage, concept, duplication, and memory."[40]

As Stanley Moses aptly observes in his discussion of the "learning force,"

> these factors are essentially the same obstacles which affect all attempts to assess the universe of adult education. This [list of factors] refers to the definition of who is an adult (as regards age or other delineators of status), the conceptual approach as to what defines an educational activity, double counting which results from the tendency of people to take more than one course, and the errors in survey and response resulting from people tending to forget and misstate activities which occurred other than in the very recent past.[41]

Free Universities

Originating as radical, counterculture alternatives to conventional college instruction in the mid-1960s, the free universities have grown from a population of one (Berkeley in 1964) to 146 in 1978, when student registrations totaled 298,255 (almost 200,000 individuals), according to a recent NCES report.[42] Although most institutions are no longer free, they remain committed to offering programs at the lowest possible charge. Based on the premise that "anyone can learn and anyone can teach," these institutions (two-thirds of which were founded after 1971) typically offer a wide range of courses to the community-at-large with no grades, credits, or other formal credentials. Teachers are recruited, usually on a volunteer or part-time basis, courses and classroom locations are publicized through a catalog, and students are registered usually at a small fee.

In addition to free universities, the NCES study identified 24 campus learning referral centers that in 1978 served 21,480 students by providing information about teaching, skill training, and tutorial services. These include the innovative "learning exchanges," telephone referral services which put people who are interested in learning about a particular topic in touch with people interested in teaching about that topic, after which the two parties work out all further arrangements. According to Peterson et al., "the free universities and learning exchanges are both extremely important models for serving the vast numbers of learners who are not motivated by the desire for credits and credentials."[43]

Correspondence Instruction

Students Enrolled in Correspondence Instruction in 1973

National Home Study Council member schools	1,062,749
Other private schools	245,687

Federal and military	1,871,978
Colleges & universities	393,741
Religious organizations	317,458
Business/industry	28,237
	3,919,850

Source: National Home Study Council, 1973

Correspondence instruction refers to all programs of education or training undertaken through the mails, whether on an individual basis or as part of an institutional setting. Correspondence courses provide individuals without access to or interest in formal education an opportunity to engage in self-directed programs of instruction which may or may not result in some form of accreditation or certification. Among the most popular subjects offered through correspondence are business, high school equivalency courses, electronics, engineering, other technical and trade areas, and art.

Correspondence learning cuts across the boundaries of education and training opportunities offered by other organizations discussed in this chapter. Among those groups making use of correspondence instruction to serve a varied and far-flung clientele are colleges and universities, the federal government and the military, and professional and community organizations.

According to a 1973 survey conducted by the National Home Study Council of institutions offering correspondence courses, there are approximately four million correspondence students in the U.S.: 67 percent enrolled in private schools, 6 percent in federal and military programs, 21 percent in colleges and universities, 3 percent in religious schools, and 3 percent in business and industry programs. But according to the 1975 NCES adult education survey, only 606,000 individuals indicated that they were participating in courses sponsored by a correspondence school. (Some of the discrepancy may be due to differing definitions in each survey as to what constitutes a correspondence school or course.) The Council estimates those schools not responding to its 1973 study have enrollments of approximately 300,000 and that an additional 105,000 students are enrolled in noncredit agricultural and homemaking courses at land-grant colleges. These two sources bring the total estimate to 4,324,850. A 1978 study of its member institutions by the National Home Study Council determined that the average NHSC student is between 25 and 34 years old, that three out of every four students are male, and that the courses offered typically require twelve months to complete and have primarily vocational objectives.

Private Instruction

The 1975 NCES survey revealed that 1,184,000 participants in adult education chose to study with a tutor or private instructor. These instructors include "paid experts" (professionals for whose services fees are charged) as well as "experts who are also a [*sic*] friend or relative." In fact, it is most probable that the latter category supplies the largest number of tutors, given that Penland's 1977 survey of self-planned learning found that the "expert who was also a friend or relative was cited as the most important source that learners and nonlearners alike sought when they wanted to know something or get information on a subject."[44] Most information obtained from the expert-friend or expert-relative is free of charge. This private instruction option is one frequently favored by older adult learners, who may be particularly hesitant to participate in a more formal, institutional learning situation with a majority of younger students.

* * * *

This is the structure of education and training opportunity for adults and workers, or at least this is what is known of it. The opportunities probably exceed what anyone thought existed, but are meager compared to what adults could use granted the opportunity in the right place at the right time with the necessary resources. But more about this in later chapters.

Do we know enough about what now exists to assess the adequacy of public and private education and training policy? Because there are lots of pieces to the puzzle, we are not sure whether some may be missing or if our arrangement constitutes an accurate picture of reality.

We recommend:

1. That responsibility lodge somewhere for putting this mosaic together every few years, in consistent fashion, so that we can see what the trends are over time and how the reality compares with our perceptions.

2. That there be appointed a National Commission on Education and Training statistics paralleling the mission of the recent National Commission on Employment Statistics. It would be the function of the Commission to identify gaps in statistical information and create surveys and studies, complementary even though sometimes carried out by different agencies, to assemble a picture of the whole as well as the parts. We measure the "labor force" regularly and consistently. We need a parallel concept of an "education and training force." As was recommended in 1975 by Willard Wirtz and Harold Goldstein, this task

should be carried out jointly by the Department of Education and the Department of Labor.[45]

3. That, however this effort is structured, there be continuing involvement of employer and union representatives as well as educators and statistical experts, so as to achieve broad coverage of instructional settings.

In this country, we only act upon what we measure, so an adequate structure of worklife education and training opportunity is unlikely to receive serious national attention until a decision is made to track what we have and how it is changing. Knowing only that somewhere between 38 and 84 million people are engaged in organized learning is just not good enough.

Notes

[1] Ruth L. Boaz, *Participation in Adult Education, Final Report 1975,* U.S. Department of Health, Education and Welfare, Washington, D.C.: Government Printing Office, 1978.

[2] Allen Tough, *The Adults' Learning Projects: A Fresh Approach to Theory and Practice in Adult Learning,* Toronto: Ontario Institute for Studies in Education, 1971; Patrick R. Penland, *Self-Planned Learning in America,* Pittsburgh: University of Pittsburgh, 1977.

[3] R. E. Peterson, K. P. Corss, S. A. Powell, T. W. Hartle, and M. A. Kutner, *Toward Lifelong Learning in America: A Sourcebook for Planners,* prepublication copy, Berkeley, Ca.: Educational Testing Service, 1978. We have drawn heavily on the typology of learning developed by the authors but using all of the most recent available estimates in each category, although we have limited our survey to deliberate learning only. The ETS effort resulted in an estimate that there are "a total of some 116 million deliberate learners in the United States." If we exclude the 42 million engaged in compulsory education and the 10 million enrolled in preprimary education, as well as the 11 million largely younger people in undergraduate, graduate, and professional education, there remain 53 million learners in the mostly work period of life.

[4] Peterson et al., Section I, p. 9.

[5] Alexis de Tocqueville, *Democracy in America,* Vintage Press, 1945, I, p. 329.

[6] Henry Adams, *The Education of Henry Adams,* first published in 1918; Time Inc., 1963, I, p. 3.

[7] GED Testing Service of the American Council on Education, *The GED Statistical Report, 1977,* Washington, D.C.: ACE, 1977.

[8] National Center for Education Statistics (NCES), *The Condition of Education,* 1979, Washington, D.C.: Government Printing Office, p. 174.

[9] According to the figures from the 1975 NCES Survey of individuals, more adult participants were enrolled in public vocational, trade, business, and flight schools than in their private counterparts. However, the 1978 NCES survey of enrollments in programs in noncollegiate postsecondary schools found just the opposite. Out of a total enrollment of 1,170,328 students, 819,940 participants were enrolled in private institutions while only 350,388 were enrolled in public institutions, despite the fact that tuition rates in private schools are five times those for public schools. This seeming contradiction is due to two major differences in the surveys. First, the 1975 study surveyed *individuals,* the 1978 study, *institutions,* and second, the surveys used different definitions. The 1975 survey included "vocational, trade, business, or flight schools,"

while the definition of noncollegiate postsecondary schools with occupational programs in 1978 included schools classified as "vocational/technical, technical institute, business/commercial, cosmetology/barber, flight, trade, arts/design, hospital, allied health, and other."

To confound matters even more, a third NCES report places noncollegiate postsecondary enrollments at 3,006,000 in October 1976, a number far out of line with the other two. This survey was of individuals, and information on student characteristics is available. Sixty percent of the women and more than 80 percent of the men were also employed full-time, and 55 percent of all the employed enrollees were both working full-time and attending school full-time. This finding suggests that considering adult education a part-time endeavor is outdated, and may account for much of the discrepancy between this survey and the 1975 survey, which looked only at part-time enrollment.

10 Wellford W. Wilms, *The Effectiveness of Public and Proprietary Occupational Training,* prepared for the National Institute of Education, Berkeley, Calif., 1974.

11 George Nolfi, "The Lifelong Learning Marketplace," paper prepared for the HEW/OE Lifelong Learning Project, Wash., D.C., 1977.

12 Otto Koester, "Occupational Education at the Postsecondary Level—Future Markets and Federal Policy Options," in *Higher Education in the 1980s: Declining Enrollments, New Markets and the Management of Decline,* Center for Educational Policy, Duke University, May 1979, pp. 94–112.

13 *The Digest of Education Statistics 1977–78,* Washington, D.C.: Government Printing Office, 1978.

14 Edmund J. Gleazer, Jr., "Testimony on Alternative Missions for Higher Education in the 80s," prepared for the U.S. Senate Committee on Labor and Human Resources, June 7, 1979.

15 Eleanor P. Godfrey and Engin I. Holmstrom, *Study of Community Colleges and Vocational-Technical Centers,* Phase I, Washington, D.C.: Bureau of Social Science Research, Inc., 1970.

16 NCES, *The Condition of Education,* 1979, Washington, D.C.: Government Printing Office, 1979.

17 Fred Harvey Harrington, *The Future of Adult Education,* San Francisco: Jossey-Bass, 1977, p. 11.

18 Florence B. Kemp, *Continuing Education: Noncredit Activities in Institutions of Higher Education,* 1975–76, USDHEW, NCES, Washington, D.C.: Government Printing Office, 1977.

19 Peterson et al.

20 Seymour Lusterman, *Education in Industry,* New York: The Conference Board, 1977.

21 James H. Neary, "The BLS Pilot Survey of Training in Industry," *Monthly Labor Review,* 97 (February 1974), 26–32.

22 Thomas F. Gilbert, "The High Cost of Knowledge," *Personnel Magazine,* March/April 1976; 9–23; Harold Goldstein, *Training Provided by Industry,* Washington, D.C.: National Manpower Institute, American Society for Training and Development, *National Report for Training and Development,* 5, no. 11, 1979.

23 David A. Smith, *An Overview of Training in the Public Sector,* Arlington, Va.: The Analytic Sciences Corporation, June 6, 1979.

24 Peterson et al.

25 Peterson et al.

26 C. Seaton, *Report on Formal Instructional Programs by Business, Industry, Government and Military in California,* Sacramento, Ca.: California Postsecondary Education Commission, 1977.

27 C. A. Brown, "Municipal Training Programs: 1975," *Urban Data Service Reports No. 8,* International City Management Association, 1976.

28 U.S. Budget, Special Analysis, 1978, p. 187.

29 *Daily Labor Report,* January 3, 1975, p. 16. The Act specifies that, wherever possible, training

should be provided on the job. Types of training provided are similar to those provided under CETA, such as machine-tool, welding, secretarial, electronics, clerical, and LPN. These training slots are approved by local employment service staff on an individual referral basis and vary with labor market demands.

30 U.S. Department of Agriculture Extension Service, *Cooperative Extension Service Programs: A Unique Experience,* Washington, D.C., 1976, p. 17.

31 Stanley M. Greenwald, "Survey of Professional Society Continuing Education Programs," Xeroxed, 1977. The survey yielded 57 responses (out of 100 inquiries), including all the major engineering and technical societies in the United States and Canada. Those societies that indicated a program in the operational or developmental stages represented approximately one million members. Taking into account duplication of memberships, approximately 565,000, or 50 percent of the total number of engineers in the U.S., hold memberships in societies that are conducting or developing continuing education programs. Approximately 1,100 courses, of one to three days in duration, were offered to about 30,000 attendees, only 45 percent of whom were members of the sponsoring organizations. Cooperative arrangements with other societies, universities, and proprietary organizations were often made to assist in the presentation of programs. The survey concludes that there is "a substantial level of continuing education activity within these organizations" and that "the goals of most organizations include the expansion of continuing education in order to meet the current and future challenges of technical change."

32 Peterson et al., Section I, p. 26.

33 Greenwald, p. 1.

34 *Employment and Training Report of the President,* 1978, p. 371.

35 Peterson et al., and telephone conversation with Sol Swerdloff of Manpower and Education Research Associates, 1979.

36 Ivan Charner, *Patterns of Adult Participation in Learning Activities,* Washington, D.C.: National Manpower Institute, forthcoming.

37 William Abbott, "College/Labor Union Cooperation," *Community and Junior College Journal,* April 1977.

38 Jane Shore, *The Education Fund of District Council 37: A Case Study,* Washington, D.C.: National Manpower Institute, September 1979.

39 Charner, op. cit.

40 NCES, *Adult Education in Community Organizations,* Washington, D.C., GPO, 1974, p. 59.

41 Stanley Moses, "The Learning Force: 1975," Xeroxed, submitted in fullfillment of a contract with the Division of Adult Education, Office of Education, August 1975.

42 NCES, *Free Universities and Learning Referral* Centers, Washington, D.C., GPO, 1978.

43 Peterson et al., Section I, pp. 50–51.

44 Penland, pp. 46–47.

45 Willard Wirtz and Harold Goldstein, *A Critical Look at the Measuring of Work,* National Manpower Institute Washington, D.C., 1975.

Chapter 3

Pattern of Participation

Those who have been successful and happy in traditional education and have pursued it to higher levels seek more of the same.

National Institute of Education, 1979

At the present time, adult education is probably more elitist on socio-economic indicators than today's undergraduate education and that may surprise some people who still think of night school as a lower class immigrants' college.

Patricia Cross, *The Adult Learner,* 1978

On the one hand,

The world of work today is the product of a hundred years of *"deskilling"*—why take the trouble to let people acquire the skills of craftsmanship when all that is wanted is the patience of a machine minder?

E. F. Schumacher, "Good Work," 1977

And on the other,

The relevance of education to work will not be its utility for jobs. It will be what it has always been—valuable in letting the disciplines of knowing have their play and their effect on the quality of reflection in the disciplines of life.

Thomas Green, "Ironies and Paradoxes," 1977

37

Our estimate of the number of adults engaged in organized learning (see Chapter 2) immediately evokes these questions: Who are these adults? Who has access to and takes advantage of these learning opportunities? And if we have answers to these questions, then what standards or principles should we apply to judging the pattern of participation we find? The pursuit of these answers begins with some fairly standard statistical exercises but leads down a path narrowing into a bramble of important philosophical and practical questions, such as whether justice is being served and whether equality of educational opportunity is being achieved.

The facts are, for a change, pretty clear and well expressed in the findings reported by the National Institute of Education (NIE) and Cross: those who have the most education are getting more of it. It would appear simple enough to conclude from this that we must aim for a more uniform distribution of participation and do whatever is necessary to see that those who had the least education in their youth have the greatest exposure to opportunity in the adult years. Shedding a few qualifications and caveats, this is in fact the conclusion of those who collaborated to write this book. If the conclusion is clear, the considerations that lead there are not. Some of the complexities are introduced by economist/philosopher Schumacher and educational philosopher Green in the quotations above. In the context of worklife education and training, how much more education and training do workers who are not now participating really need in our modern industrial economy? And is further education still worthwhile, even if they don't need it for work?

We must first understand the pattern of participation and then examine what this pattern may mean for public and private policy. Who does and does not participate in education and training? Why and why not? Should there be an effort to change the pattern of participation, and what might that mean on a practical basis?

Who Does and Who Doesn't

To answer the question of who does and does not participate in education and training programs, we must rely heavily on one national survey of adult education that has provided details about participation since 1969 at about three-year intervals. As a comprehensive measure of adult education, this survey has shortcomings, as discussed in the preceding chapter. But it does quite a good job of showing *differences* in participation, if it does miss the mark in measuring the *levels*. Although preliminary data have just become available for 1978, all the published analysis has been of the period ending in 1975. By this measure, 11.6 percent of the adult population participated in education or training in 1978, exactly the same percentage as in 1975.[1]

In the last two decades, the nation has experienced substantial growth in adult education participation. The percentage of adults so engaged advanced from 7.6 percent in 1957 to 10 percent in 1969 and then to 11.3 percent in 1972. By the 1975 survey, participation had begun to level off at 11.6 percent, prompting many observers to wonder whether the growth period was over. The 1978 statistics showed no further growth, except that resulting from the increase in population from 1975 to 1978. Given the NCES definition of adult learning—much more limited than that used in Chapter 2—we cannot be sure that organized learning has in fact stopped growing. All we can say is that the part-time, school-related portion probably has. But again, we look to the NCES surveys mainly to identify *differences* in participation tendencies among various population groups.

The most striking variation in participation is among adults with different *levels* of education. Among those with less than high school educations, only 3.3 percent participated in 1978 compared to 26.5 percent of those with four or more years of college. In between those groups, 11.1 percent of high school graduates participated, as did 17.5 percent of those with from one to three years of college. This pattern of participation has been practically unchanged since 1969; the growth in the total rate has been due to a growth in the proportion of the population with higher levels of education. This pattern is confirmed by a number of other studies.

It is not so surprising that people who had the most education when young are those who want more when they get older. People who play the piano when young are more likely to do so at age forty and people who ski when young are more likely to continue to do so and we don't think very much about it. But the amount of education one has had is very much interrelated with where one is in the occupational structure and thereby with level of income. As we expand educational opportunity, it is important to be aware that differential participation will have some effect on success in other areas of life. And to the extent that educational opportunity is supplied through public policies, it is necessary to ask whether those policies promote equal access and whether they promote economic and social equality, or whether they contribute to inequality.

Younger people are more likely to participate in education and training opportunities. In study after study, age emerges as a principal difference between participants and nonparticipants. Some of this difference is due simply to the fact that older people have less education and people with less education have lower participation rates. But studies that have held education constant still show substantial age differences. Among those 17 to 34, 15.5 percent participated in 1978, as did 12.9 percent of those 35 to 55. The real difference is with those 55 and over, of whom only 4.4 percent participated. While this general pattern has been seen in all surveys since 1969, there is one significant change. The participation rate for those 55 and over, though still low, has been rising steadily. In 1969, it was 2.9 percent, going to 3.5 percent in 1972, to 4.0 percent in 1975, to 4.4 percent in 1978. This is an encouraging trend to those who see education and training as one important approach to occupational adjustment and the rewarding use of leisure time in later life.

The differences in the trends of participation on the basis of race are not encouraging, at least with respect to blacks. The participation rate for black adults is 6.5 percent, compared to 12.2 percent for whites. More worrisome than the absolute difference is the fact that the rate for blacks has been declining slowly but steadily from 7.8 percent in 1969. To whatever extent education and training can help adult blacks catch up to whites in the occupational structure, the current trend is in the wrong direction from the standpoint of national policy objectives. The reasons underlying this lower and declining rate should be carefully identified to see if some special effort could reverse this downward trend. The combined rate for other races is actually higher than the rate for whites, and from 1969 to 1975 was increasing. There was a decline in 1978, however, to 12.7 percent from the 1975 high of 13.4 percent.

The statistics also show an elimination of the gap between men and women. The female participation rate has been advancing in each survey, and in 1978 reached 12.5 percent, higher than the male rate of 11.3 percent. This is a reversal of the situation in 1969 when the rate for females was 9.9 percent, compared to 11.2 percent for males. It would be worth finding out whether participation by women is also associated with occupational advancement. If it is, then a continuation of these trends will be an important factor in achieving worklife equality between the sexes.

From the standpoint of occupational equality, it is necessary to look behind the gross figures to see what kind of education and training women have access to. One obvious conclusion is that since women are underrepresented in the jobs that have the best benefits, they are less likely to have access to education and training available through the workplace. The jobs they are likely to have are those that require less training, with the result, as the NIE has found, that "employer-sponsored programs . . . are still relatively closed to women, with men's participation rate . . . double that of women."[2]

Given the pattern of participation by educational level, it is not surprising that there is also a considerable difference in participation among different income levels. At incomes of under $5,000, only 5.3 percent participate. This rises by income level to 17.5 percent for people making $25,000 or more. This pattern has held in all four surveys that have been conducted. By occupation, blue-collar operatives and farmers have the lowest participation rates, white-collar workers are in the mid-range, and professional and technical workers have the highest rates—over one out of three in 1975. Such statistics, of course, raise the question of what role adult education and training plays in achieving these higher levels of income and occupational status and how much such behaviors just go along with the lifestyle and demands of the occupations.

Why They Do

The largest single reason adults participate in education and training is to advance in the workworld. This was true in the surveys of 1969, 1972, and 1975. In 1975, 53.3 percent said they participated in order to improve or advance in their current job or to get a new job. This is confirmed by looking at the actual courses adults take; in 1975, 49 percent were enrolled in occupational training, up from 45 percent in 1969, and very much higher than for any other kind of education or training.

One might suppose that people with the least education, who also on the average have the lowest-paying jobs, would be the most interested in using education to advance in employment. Quite the opposite is the case, for while about a fourth of those with less than ninth-grade educations and a fourth of those with less than high school educations participate for this purpose, half of all college graduates use education and training to improve or advance in a job. College graduates, however, are somewhat less likely to use education as a means of finding a new job.

While over half of white males say they use education and training to advance on the job, this is true of only three out of ten females. In terms of actual courses taken, the disparity is even greater, with 62 percent of white males enrolled in occupational training compared to just over a third of white females. Among blacks, the male and female proportions are close together, with 45 percent and 42 percent enrolled to advance in a job. The proportion of blacks using education to get a *new* job is double that of whites, and there is little difference between males and females in this regard. The lesser use of education and training by white women for employment purposes is made up for by a greater use for enrichment of social life, personal and family life, and recreation. However, there is little difference between black males and females in this respect and very few blacks of either sex view their participation as part of their social life or recreation (although one out of four white women does).

The percentage of adults enrolled in general education courses declined between the 1969 and 1975 surveys from 27 percent to 21 percent. The largest proportion of participants taking general education, by educational level, are those who have had the least education. By race and sex, the greatest enrollment in general education is among black females. Courses that concern "community issues," rather than work advancement or general education, attract about one in ten adults. The less educated are more likely to enroll than those with advanced educations, and whites more likely than blacks.

It is likely that the people designing the surveys from which we have extracted our "pattern" determine the answers to such questions as "Why did you enroll in education or training?" about as much as do the students answering them. Lists of reasons for participation are placed before the students and they are asked to choose one or more. If a lot of people go back to school because of some vague feeling of incompleteness in their present life routines, those vague feelings will not be picked up in surveys of the kind reported here. A recent survey of workers conducted by the National Manpower Institute included the choice "to become a well-rounded person." This apparently sounded like the best reason of all and was subscribed to by 86 percent, with "improving job performance" running a close second. All surveys have their shortcomings, giving more a glimpse of the truth than an unobstructed view.

Why They Don't

There is some information from surveys about why adults don't enroll in education and training programs. It is probably less reliable than the data on why people do. Where the opportunity exists and is accessible, where time and money are available, a person may have confronted the opportunity thoughtfully and decided against it for conscious reasons. If the surveyor has the right box to check on the form, there is prospect of getting a reasonably reliable answer. There are also some individuals who are quite clear about what education they want and why, and about what stands in their way. They, too, will give useful answers to our questions.

But many more people will not have reached judgments on which we can predict or explain behavior, perhaps because opportunities for education don't exist or they are unaware of them. As Patricia Cross has said, "People can't make valid judgments until they see and experience the alternatives to the familiar. In short, survey respondents seem somewhat more prone to like what they know than to know what they like."[3]

In ascertaining the reasons adults don't participate, there is also the problem that since education is generally highly regarded by our society, people sometimes tend to put the best face on decisions not to take advantage of education and training opportunities. Some inkling of this factor at work can be gleaned from a survey that asked both why the respondent did not participate *and* why the respondent thought *other* people did not participate. While only 2 percent attributed "lack of interest" to themselves, 26 percent attributed lack of interest to others.[4] People may hesitate simply to say, "I am not interested."

Nevertheless, a number of surveys have tried to identify reasons for nonparticipation or barriers to participation, with some fairly consistent results. A summary of the results of most of these surveys can be found in the National

Manpower Institute monograph *Patterns of Adult Participation in Learning Activities,* by Ivan Charner. The reasons most frequently given for not participating are cost and time. Patricia Cross estimates that about one-third of all adults report that these two factors are obstacles to participation.[5] A study of blue-collar workers reports 48 percent finding tuition costs a barrier and 31 percent not having enough time.[6] In another study of would-be learners, 53 percent reported costs and 46 percent reported time as barriers.[7] In a sample of blue-collar workers eligible for tuition aid, about a fourth said cost was a problem and a third cited lack of time.[8] On the other hand, other observers of adult workers conclude that the major reason they don't participate is just lack of interest, and the question remains as to how well survey responses reflect real reasons.

Although less clear, there are also barriers to participation that grow out of self-perception. In two studies, 12 percent and 18 percent reported a lack of confidence in ability and 17 percent and 21 percent believed themselves too old to go back to school.[9] Women more frequently than men report that they feel too old to go back and men more frequently cite lack of confidence. Younger workers more often report lack of confidence than do older workers. But the differences among different groups of workers on such "state of mind" factors is not large.

There are special problems and considerations affecting that large group of workers in hourly wage jobs on production lines or other unskilled jobs where there seem to be few avenues of job advancement. There are even larger problems faced by working women in the lower-paid and often sex-stereotyped jobs, particularly if they have families.

An unusually penetrating insight into the problems of working women was gained through a survey conducted in women's magazines by the National Commission on Working Women (NCWW). Tabulations were made for 110,-000 out of 150,000 questionnaires returned. A principal finding was that working women still do double duty, an eight-hour job plus regular family and household responsibilities. Nearly half of all employed respondents expressed a problem, put this way by a woman in Tacoma, Washington:

> Work has increasingly become a place you go that takes the entire day and have to leave each evening to go to Job 2—Chef, Maid, Housekeeper, and Nanny.[10]

Complicating the problem of working women with families is the inadequacy of arrangements for child care. Among working women in the survey, one-third reported that child care arrangements were still a problem. The adequacy of child care is also a factor heavily influencing participation in education. This lack of leisure time and inadequacy of child care caused about 40 percent of women in the NCWW survey (44,000 in the survey alone) to say they had no time to continue their education. In addition, 36 percent indicated they had no chance to train for a better job. Despite such obstacles, women's overall participation in education and training has been rising (although women are more likely than men to be using the education for nonoccupational purposes). Most likely, however, this increase is coming among women who already have the best educations and the best jobs. The NCWW survey found that twice as many nonprofessional women found barriers to education and training as did women in professional jobs. Yet education and training may be critical to make the jump, as it is for a San Diego, California, woman: "I am currently near the top of my field as an Executive Secretary and feel I should have plans to do something else. . . . My solution at this point is to attend night school at the Community College to try to figure out what even interests me."

The male blue-collar worker and his family will, of course, have a different view of the educational world than a working women, and because blue-collar participation rates are so low, we need to look especially closely at why. In fact, in the blue-collar culture there is more likely to be resistance to changing roles for women and more comfort with sharply different sex roles. It is true that, for the male blue-collar worker, education is the ever-beckoning "door to opportunity"; it may also be the sieve and the winnower that bruised him badly when he was young.

There are no hard-and-fast lines defining different lifestyles for people of different occupational groupings, but there are important differences in central tendencies. If our intent is to reengage the blue-collar worker in education or training activities, we will have to formulate policies and programs that take into account not only a frequent ambivalence toward schooling but also the whole complex of attitudes, values, and preferred activities common in blue-collar culture.

Let us review briefly the aspects of that culture that appear most salient for any formulation of an education and training policy addressed to this group of workers. Perhaps the most crucial aspect to be taken into account is economic situation—a situation of chronic anxiety and insecurity. In plain language, many of these workers simply do not have the money to spend on further education (unless, of course, aid is provided by their employer or their union). Related to their financial situation is the fact that many of them have little opportunity for advancement on their jobs and thus see little *economic* advantage to be gained from investing their limited financial resources in further education. An attitudinal factor that enters here is the fact that, for most blue-collar workers, education is seen mainly as an economic tool. For both themselves and their children, education is valued primarily for vocational purposes.[11]

Leisure time, like work time, is often spent in physical activities which do not require education for their performance or enjoyment. Moreover, the notion of education for self-development is not as familiar to blue-collar workers and their families as it is to other economic groups.

A tendency toward isolation from broader community life makes it more difficult for the male blue-collar worker to take a step toward education, even if he wants to. Instances are cited of men who attempted to improve their position but lack the resources for doing so. Their isolation from [community] institutions limits utilization even of such assistance as the community provides.[12] The workplace, the union, the church, and, for some, the fraternal order are the institutions that regularly touch the lives of blue-collar workers. If the news of educational opportunity is to reach them, a lot of it will have to come through such familiar channels.

The studies reviewed here consistently make the point that blue-collar men and women are often ambivalent about many of the values and attitudes that are considered "mainstream." This is particularly true of attitudes toward sex roles, child-rearing, the meaning and purpose of work, and the value of education (at least for themselves; they will urge their children to go to college). Since educational institutions, particularly postsecondary institutions, are the primary carriers of these "mainstream" attitudes and values, they often may not be perceived by blue-collar men and women as offering relevant or desirable experiences. Going to college may even be seen by some as an experience that will threaten or attack their way of life and their values. These attitudes, rooted in work and family experiences, pose barriers to efforts to engage blue-collar workers in traditional postsecondary education. Efforts in this direction may lead educators to examine their assumptions about what education is or could be for students with widely varied life and work experiences.

The provision of educational and career counseling is increasingly being proposed as a way to help workers make the transition from work back to education. However, for this counseling to be effective, it must be undertaken with well-informed sensitivity to the workers it is intended to help, for studies of blue-collar workers suggest that they may be inhibited from revealing—even to their spouses—feelings of weakness, inadequacy, or fear. According to Komarovsky, emotions are not often named and reflected upon and what follows from this is a lack of interest and confidence in talking as therapeutic or leading to anything.[13] These cultural facts require a particular counseling approach, one that does not invade the worker's emotional territory or threaten a sense of identity.

If the counseling approach is to succeed, new counseling methods that incorporate and build upon the values and strengths of the blue-collar culture will need to be developed. A few examples of promising new approaches do exist. AFSCME's District Council 37 Education Fund in New York City has developed a counseling program that is highly subscribed and apparently well received by the workers it serves. At DC 37, the counseling is integrated as much as possible into the regular classroom situation to avoid any implication that educational and career counseling is "therapy." The counseling itself focuses on very practical, work-related issues: what education or training is necessary to keep the job I have now; what do I need to do to get my high school diploma; what will I need to learn to pass the next Civil Service test? In addition, the counseling approach focuses on the *family unit* rather than the individual and seeks to help the worker anticipate and deal with the effects on family life that may arise from going back to school. The counselors themselves are chosen in part on the basis of their affinity with the people they will counsel; most of them returned to education as adults and are familiar with the experiences and values that have shaped their clients' views and feelings about education.[14]

Factors producing nonparticipation, beyond the general life situation workers find themselves in, include institutional practices that appear to stand in the way of education and training. Some policies, practices, and rhetoric of employer and educational institutions have the effect of excluding or discouraging adult workers from participating in learning programs. Institutional factors can be grouped into five problem areas: scheduling, location/transportation, lack of courses, application and approval procedures, and information. Of these, location, scheduling, and lack of interesting or relevant courses are most often mentioned as barriers to learning.

A review of studies of the needs and attitudes of adult learners found that generally, one-fourth of all survey respondents reported these as barriers to their participation.[15]

With respect to information, one study found 10 percent of would-be learners reporting lack of information as a barrier.[16] When different groups of workers are looked at, however, the findings differ. Lack of information was cited by 18 percent of blue-collar workers[17] and 42.6 percent of unionized workers. In addition, 43.6 percent of unionized workers reported they lacked information about their negotiated tuition-aid program. In one study that asked about counseling, 50.7 percent felt they did not receive enough counseling about what courses were available and whether they were qualified to take them.[18]

Despite the fact that between 10 percent and 40 percent of adults cite lack of information as a barrier, there is evidence that many more have inadequate information about available options. As Cross suggests, "One wonders if many perceived problems with schedules, locations, and courses are not ultimately due to lack of information about the options that do exist."[19]

Now that more educational institutions are rapidly responding to the barriers of scheduling, location, and courses, the most neglected institutional barriers are lack of information and inadequate counseling. And as more options become available, the importance of these two factors will increase.

Closing Opportunity Gaps

In the 1970s the nontraditional learner was discovered, or rediscovered, according to Fred Harvey Harrington. The phrase "stop out" was introduced by the Carnegie Commission on Higher Education and "considered break" by Willard Wirtz; academic credit for "noncollegiate education" was recognized by the American Council on Education; credit for life and work experiences became available through the Council for Advancement of Experiential Learning; the idea of "nonresident students" was modeled on the U.K.'s Open University and the U.S.'s Goddard College; and a so-far lifeless Lifelong Learning Act was passed by the Congress at mid-decade. Adult enrollments surged, particularly in the first part of the decade, and then settled into a gradual pattern of growth.

A sobering assessment with which to begin the 1980s is that this early growth was fed by the food in the seed pod and now that the plant is above ground, it must endure the elements and be watered and fertilized regularly. The first concern is that this growth has been quite uneven and the larger numbers have not much changed the underlying patterns of participation.

There is, to be sure, considerable achievement in the learning efforts of women as compared to men, although there is still considerable disparity in the kind of education and training women get. But there is reason for alarm in the downward trend in the participation of black adults, as against the gradual rise for white. Will this trend make parity of occupation and income harder to obtain? This downward trend is offset by the fact that blacks more frequently use their adult education for an occupational objective.

If not alarming, it is, nevertheless, disturbing that there has been practically no change over the decade in the participation of adults with different educational levels. As we push to even higher levels of participation, what does it mean that 27 percent of college graduates participate, as compared to only 3 percent of people who do not have a high school education?

It would be a mistake to follow a direction in which public policies contribute to any widening of socioeconomic cleavages. But it would be a worse mistake to stop the growth of adult education and training opportunity because its use is uneven in the society. Herein lies a dilemma.

The present pattern of greater use by the higher socioeconomic groups is not, in our own analysis, a matter fixed in the stars. Instead it is probably the natural result of the ad hoc way we have grafted adult education onto a system basically designed to educate youth. The institutions that attract youth to their campuses offer what those youth want, and so the affinity between educational institutions and their traditional clientele perpetuates a familiar pattern into adult life. And at the workplace, those occupations that require considerable education to enter also seem to offer or encourage more education to continue or advance in them.

The sum of it is that the college campus isn't seeking a 40-year-old truck driver who didn't finish the tenth grade and the college campus seems even more remote to the truck driver at age 40 than it did at age 16. And at work, the company may want a bookkeeper to become an accountant, but isn't much concerned that the trucker do more than stick to the schedule and the road. An inner-city black may be picking up odd jobs and would consider elevation to trucking a big step up—particularly with the romanticizing of the free life of the road in the late 1970s—but doesn't see any link between going back to school and getting a trucking job.

At the same time that we need to keep what momentum the '70s produced going in terms of expanding opportunity, we need to concentrate on finding avenues that lead to opportunity for all races, both sexes, and those who were unenthusiastic about the learning system they encountered when they were young. We suspect this will require coming to grips with the observations of both Schumacher and Green, that we must find as many connections as we can between further learning and occupational advancement (proving we want more than just patient machine minders); at the same time we must recognize the larger value learning has that goes far beyond utility for jobs. Doing this, however, means moving very quickly from this philosophical plane to that of acquiring real experience with successful ways to equalize access to adult learning opportunity. There are, in several chapters of this volume, recommendations that would widen opportunity for those groups that now have medium to low participation rates, and they need not be detailed here. There are, however, a number of public and private actions that would give content to an objective of broadened participation and are worth mentioning or worth repeating.

- A process of local collaboration among education institutions, employers, unions, and local government will broaden the information base of education institutions and enable them to be more responsive to the learning needs of a broad range of adults with different educational backgrounds and occupational experiences.

- More systematic attention to the use of training and education in private industry to make the workforce as productive as possible would tend to broaden the base of adult learning in the employment context where workers are likely to see the largest connection between learning and employment opportunity.

- The employment and training programs of the Comprehensive Employment and Training Act target their efforts on low income people who have the least education. These programs fund basic education and job training opportunities. But they do not provide the information, brokering, and advisement services that would link these adults to the whole of educational opportunity in the community and not just to those classroom slots created by CETA. This linking could be done on a demonstration basis in several cities through joint efforts by the local educational brokering agency and the CETA prime sponsor. It would extend to low-income employed people as well as the unemployed and to the WIN program for people on welfare as well as the regular CETA-eligible population.

- Another means of approaching equality of access is to get information and educational advisement services into channels where there is contact with populations that now have low participation rates. Recommendations for doing this are made in more detail in Chapter 4, but are summarized below:

  — One or two demonstration programs run by each international union, providing educational information and brokering services
  — Several pilot programs in which information about education and training opportunity is provided through neighborhood associations, which have grown in number and are frequently in lower-income and working-class neighborhoods
  — Pilot programs in public Employment Service offices to make referrals to educational information and brokering agencies or to have the information available within the office, possibly through outstationing of personnel from local educational brokering agencies
  — Greater direct provision of educational information services and counseling at the place of employment where tuition-aid programs are available. Small-scale testing in a few sites is presently under way (see Chapter 10 for more detail)

- As Basic Opportunity Grants are liberalized to accommodate more adult part-time students, there should be a policy of getting the information about their availability and application procedures before the widest possible adult audience. Otherwise, there will be a tendency for the information to go through the kinds of channels that better-educated adults are already plugged into. The channels of the Department of Labor could be used here, through the Occupational Safety and Health

Administration (OSHA), the CETA prime sponsors, and the 2,800 offices of the United States Employment Service.

- Beyond the information and counseling barriers that exist for people with little education and low incomes, there are other possible impediments to achieving a more equal participation in education and training. But they are not going to be identified through questionnaires with enough sureness to warrant expenditure of resources to remove them. There needs, instead, to be a base in experience for judging what actually changes participation and what doesn't. To establish such a base will require a substantial experimentation and demonstration program. A few possibilities include:

  — Workplace experiments in which policies of flextime enable workers to take advantage of education and training opportunities in the community
  — A variety of approaches to child care problems specifically geared to women who are kept from education and training by family responsibilities
  — Installment plan or deferred payment arrangements for paying tuition, where lump-sum payment in advance is preventing enrollment
  — Adjustment in scheduling and location of course offerings to fit times adults have available and places they are comfortable being
  — Assessment of worker competencies for academic credit to give them a headstart on long part-time degree programs.

- In general, where public funds are expended to fund adult and employee participation in education and training, there should be a required plan or strategy (like a marketing plan) for achieving the broadest possible participation and for attempting to reach people who are not already college graduates, workers with high incomes, or professional employees.

* * * *

The United States cannot accept its system of adult learning becoming, in Patricia Cross's words, "more elitist . . . than today's undergraduate education." We should reinforce efforts to achieve the greatest possible equality of opportunity for whites and blacks, men and women, people at lower and higher rungs on the occupational ladder, and high school dropouts as well as college graduates. And if, among a relatively few, "a canine appetite for knowledge [is] generated, which must be fed," as Emerson put it, we can satisfy that appetite without ignoring that larger number who in their youth found education less tasty or were simply deprived of learning opportunities.

The 1980s seem like a very good time to work out a better pattern of participation in adult learning.

Notes

1 Ruth L. Boaz, *Participation in Adult Education: Final Report 1975,* U.S. Department of Health, Education, and Welfare, Washington, D.C.: Government Printing Office, 1978.
2 *An Evaluative Look at Nontraditional Postsecondary Education,* ed. Charles B. Stalford, National Institute of Education, Washington, D.C.: Government Printing Office, 1978, p. 14.
3 Patricia Cross, *The Adult Learner,* American Association for Higher Education, National Conference Series, 1978, p. 7.
4 J. Wilcox, R. A. Stafford, and H. D. Veres, *Continuing Education: Bridging the Information Gap,* Institute for Research and Development in Occupational Education, Ithaca, N.Y.: Cornell University, 1975.
5 Patricia Cross, "A Critical Review of State and National Studies of the Needs and Interests of Adult Learners," in *Adult Learning Needs and the Demand in Lifelong Learning,* ed. Charles Stafford, National Institute of Education, Washington, D.C., 1978.
6 P. Botsman, "The Learning Needs and Interests of Adult Blue-Collar Workers," an Extension Publication of the New York State College of Human Ecology, Ithaca, N.Y., 1975.
7 A. Carp, R. Peterson, and P. Roelfs, "Adult Learning Interests and Experiences," in Patricia Cross and John R. Valley and Associates, *Planning Non-Traditional Programs,* San Francisco: Jossey-Bass, 1976.
8 Ivan Charner et al., *An Untapped Resource: Negotiated Tuition-Aid Plans in the Private Sector,* National Manpower Institute, Washington, D.C., 1978.
9 Carp et al., and Botsman.
10 National Survey of Working Women: Perceptions, Problems, and Prospects, National Commission on Working Women, June, 1979, p. 4.
11 Mirra Komarovsky, *Blue Collar Marriage,* New York: Random House, 1964.
12 Arthur Shostak, *Blue Collar Life,* New York: Random House, 1969.
13 Komarovsky.
14 Jane Shore, *The Education Fund of District Council 37: A Case Study,* Washington, D.C.: National Manpower Institute, 1979.
15 Cross, 1978.
16 Carp et al.
17 Botsman.
18 Charner et al.
19 Cross, 1978.

Chapter 4

Making the
Right Connection

Adults are quite clear in their desire for more and better information on educational opportunities, and many want a wider range of counseling services than is now usually provided.

Patricia Cross and A. Zusman, "The Needs of
Non-Traditional Learners and Responses of
Non-Traditional Programs," 1977

The employee "counseling and guidance" or "educational advisement" procedures that are established emerge from all three successful tuition-aid programs . . . as being probably of critical importance.

Willard Wirtz, *Tuition-Aid Revisited: Tapping the
Untapped Resource,* 1979

When adult Americans are asked whether they need better information and assistance to get from work to learning or from household duties to school and then to work, they will say they do. And when three successful tuition-aid programs were studied to see what makes them work, Willard Wirtz found that adequate advice to workers was a very important ingredient. Yet very few adults wanting to learn would know where to go to get such information and counseling. Few organizations exist to meet this need, although their numbers are growing. There are also organizations with other primary missions that do, or could, provide some help here.

As we said in Chapter 2, the present system for the provision of organized learning opportunities is pluralistic and diverse. It will become more so if the kind of policies reviewed and recommended in this volume become practice. We believe there will be substantial benefit to adult citizens and employees from enlarging opportunities for learning on a wide front—in regular schools, in colleges, in union halls, at workplaces, in libraries, and so on. Only in these ways can the very different needs of adults be accommodated. But with this diversity there will have to be some way for adults to make a connection between their goals and available learning opportunities if they are to make use of the options open to them.

While there is increasing interest in adults among members of the counseling and guidance profession, that profession has mostly dealt with the young. There is quite a different set of issues involved in the problem of providing educational advisement and information to adults than there is in facilitating the movement of youth from high school to college. The colleges and universities have had almost a single source from which to get their students—the secondary school. Information about admissions and courses was funneled to students through high school counselors who were the linchpins between the high school and the college. And a standardized test, the Scholastic Aptitude Test (SAT)—at least from the college's standpoint—helped to grade and sort prospective students.

Potential adult students are not gathered in any central place. Instead, they are found in homes, offices, factories, unions, and churches. They often have very specific objectives, and need to know what kind of education will enable them to reach these objectives, and where that education can be found in the community and at the least cost in money and time. People who give good educational advice to adults have to know about the constraints working adults encounter. They must be briefed about employment and avenues of advancement, about what employers require, in order to relate an educational plan to an employment outcome. (Of course, there are other objectives besides jobs and careers, but over half of prospective adult learners will have employment objectives in mind.) And on the learning side, adult advisors must make it their business, as few have, to find *all* the learning institutions in the community and know how adults can get into them.

There are some very significant starts in grappling with just these kinds of problems of potential learners. For communities and organizations that want to help adults and workers make the best learning connection, there are some good models of community-based counseling services to consider with some good experiences to follow. And there are other multipurpose institutions and agencies with adult services that are relating to the needs of adult learners. More connecting services are needed. This chapter examines the variety of old and new linking mechanisms that play an intermediary role in helping the working person make the right connection with learning resources to fulfill personal and occupational goals, and it proposes measures to expand and improve them.

As societies become more complex, intermediary roles become critically important in many areas of life. Most people would feel confused and apprehensive going before a court of law without a well-informed lawyer as an intermediary. General practitioners in the health profession are increasingly acting as intermediaries between patients and the array of highly specialized experts no layperson could hope to select accurately. Employment services are intermediaries between would-be workers and jobs. There is no less need in the adult learning field.

The review here is of the organizations, old and new, that provide these intermediary services. At the same time, we recognize that people have an increasing interest in learning to do their own career and educational planning, and that the bookstores currently offer a number of self-planning guides, of which the best-known authors are Richard Bolles and John Crystal. We view this as a parallel and complementary development.

The United States Employment Service

The most far-reaching network of support for adults making occupational and educational decisions is to be found in the 2,836 Employment Service offices with placement services across the nation. Yet only a small percentage of people seeking opportunities for earning or learning are served by the Employment Service system.

Employment Service offices are fully funded by the U.S. Employment Service, under the Wagner-Peyser Act of 1933, by means of annual grants to state governments, which direct the services at the local level. Most of the 30,000 staff members of these offices are intake workers and interviewers whose job it is to provide a link between persons in search of work and employers in search of workers. Their task is to place people in jobs as fast as possible. There are also thousands of Employment Counselors. They, too, are under pressure to spend a short time with clients and to get them into a paying job. The way states and local services are funded—the so-called resource allocation formula —gives very heavy weight to the number of job placements made by the local service. As one experienced staff member put it, "The emphasis is on quick and easy placements to get the numbers up."

The Employment Service (ES) has gained the reputation in many quarters since the mid-1960s of being a labor exchange for the lowest-paid and the highest-turnover jobs. The ES is limited by the number of job openings listed by employers with its local offices; most openings are not listed. The number of job placements has declined since the mid-1960s, after the Department of Labor directed the Employment Service to focus on the disadvantaged, to between 5 percent and 8 percent of the total new hiring in the country. While employers are less attracted to the least employable applicants, ES, nevertheless, found jobs for over 3 million persons in the first nine months of 1977, at an estimated cost of $160 per placement.[1]

Actually, 38 percent of the new permanent job orders listed with the Employment Service are designated as low-skill, low-status occupations by the Department of Labor. They include domestic work, restaurant occupations, cleaning occupations, material handling, manual labor, service station attendant jobs, packaging, and others. In addition, there are temporary jobs for casual day laborers and domestic day workers.[2] While the largest block of placements are in these low-status occupations, there are significant numbers placed in professional, managerial, and technical occupations as well.

The basic law of the Employment Service, which has remained unchanged since its passage in the early days of the New Deal, authorizes counseling as well as placement activity, and the United States Employment Service (USES) requires that each state devote some of its resources to counseling. In the planning budget for FY 1980, for example, it is required that a minimum of 5 percent of staff time be devoted to counseling functions. It is also required that 6.2 percent of the new and renewed applicants of local services receive counseling—a figure that was the national average in 1979. Finally, the USES guidelines provide that the caseload per counselor should be between 600 and 800 individuals per year.

To carry out these counseling requirements, in September 1978, out of a total staff of 30,000, the states employed 4,313 people who were engaged in counseling functions at least part of the time. Two thousand of them spent over half their time in counseling, and the remainder, less than half of their time. Only about three-quarters of staff members providing counseling functions were in jobs classified as "employment counselors." The 3,114 staff members in these positions were divided about evenly between males and females. Their numbers represent an increase in counseling personnel, since a low in the early 1970s, thanks in part to contracts from CETA prime sponsors for assessment and advisement services to CETA clients.

From time to time, the functions and qualifications of employment counselors are redefined by the Department of Labor. The primary responsibility as defined in 1965 was to assist employable individuals to make a suitable choice for change. The emphasis was on "employable individuals."[3] In 1971, the job of the employment counselor was redirected to deal "largely with individuals who are handicapped by a wide variety of disadvantages in obtaining employment." The task was changed to helping people who were not "employable" to overcome "as many barriers as possible to employability," such as "physical, personal, and social handicaps; lack of skill training; inadequate basic education; and poor attitudes towards self, others, and the world of work."[4] The emphasis now, in other words, is on those who are "least employable," those with educational, social, and physical deficiencies. If these deficiencies are to be made up through further education and training, then the counselors need to be in the educational counseling business.

Who receives employment counseling? The clients of ES employment counselors are referred to them by ES interviewers or by outside agencies. The USES Chief of Employment Counseling, Oscar Gjernes, estimates that 40 percent of the counselees are "early entrants" to the labor force, meaning that they are seeking their first job or have not acquired enough experience and training to be above entry-level status. A pilot evaluation study of three sites by the Stanford Research Institute observed that the employment counselors received the most mentally or emotionally disturbed and least job-ready people who presented themselves for placement to the Employment Service. "Because Employment Service interviewers are evaluated on their placement record, they usually refer to counseling only those clients who are extremely poor placement prospects."[5]

There is a federal effort to raise the quality of employment counseling and enforce certification standards for staff members with the formal title of Employment Counselor. The initiative was taken by the State Employment Service in Florida, then financially supported by DOL, to develop a competency-based assessment and training program. The result is a multivolume, eighteen-month training program in eight competency areas:

1. relationship skills
2. career development
3. group counseling and guidance
4. individual and group assessment
5. community relations
6. continuity of service
7. accountability and productivity
8. professional development

In 1979–80, staff from USES trained ES state counseling supervisors and others to spread the use of the program. Is is proposed that federal certificates be awarded to those employees whom the state's ES officer judges, by federal standards, to have successfully demonstrated the required competencies. Federal certification of professional attainment would be a new and controversial departure, with the potential for widespread impact beyond the Employment Service. By the end of 1979, several state governments (including Wisconsin, Florida, Kentucky, Virginia, and Pennsylvania) had mandated the achievement of the program's competencies for employment and promotion. USES representatives were already talking to counselor trainees at Penn State and elsewhere to persuade them to follow the precedent of the University of Florida in Gainesville in adopting part or all of the program in training counselors of adults.

What adults can expect to receive what kind of job and educational linking services from the employment counselors of their local Employment Service offices? The evidence indicates that those with the greatest chance of reaching an employment counselor through the referral system are people who are experiencing significant but not insuperable problems in gaining employment. These problems can be in medical condition, training and education, or attitude and behavior. Clients can receive as many as five or six appointments with a counselor if they are assertive, but the counselor will be under pressure not to exceed by much the national average of 2.3 sessions. Counselors' capabilities will most likely include helping to develop employment plans based on clients' needs and preferences, measuring aptitudes and interests, and providing information on types of occupations as well as local job and training opportunities. The client should expect that the counselor will feel some pressure to place him or her as soon as possible in a training or education program or a job. Referrals to local training and education opportunities may be made.

Counseling under Comprehensive Employment and Training Act Programs

The most well financed sites where working people can find linkages with the training and education world are the programs funded by the Federal Comprehensive Employment and Training Act (CETA). There are 465 "prime sponsors" of programs under this act located in cities and counties with populations of over 100,000. In addition, the state government functions as prime sponsor for "the balance of the state" outside such populated areas, and they contract with local agencies (frequently the Employment Service) to carry out CETA programs. These programs are targeted on low-income, disadvantaged populations.

The CETA legislation mandates that monies spent under it be allocated 60 percent to participants, 15 percent to administrative costs, and 25 percent for staff and program. The funding of guidance services comes from the 25 percent allocation for staff and program, and does not ordinarily have a separate budget. In fact, the counseling function is very broadly interpreted and the counselor's role often requires that he/she perform intake, assessment, placement, attendance, and job development, as well as the more narrowly defined traditional counseling function of helping clients to become aware of their own needs, preferences, and skills, to make plans for future development, and to take action on them. The counselors are also called upon to intervene between CETA trainees and their teachers and employers when problems arise. These problems usually center on tardiness, absenteeism, dress code, and appropriate conduct on the job.

Counselors do have a major referral role with CETA eligibles, and key referral points are General Educational Development (GED) programs, institutions of higher education, libraries, health agencies, and the Department of Human Services. In addition, the CETA contractors are required to provide counseling for trainees, and that frequently is done not by "counselors" but by the vocational teachers, who feel closer to the participants they see each day. Many teachers only refer trainees to the counselor when problems get too tough or the trainee drops out.

As a result, counseling responsibilities are diffuse and roles poorly defined. "We are all counselors here," one staff member in Boston told a researcher. Among some prime sponsors, the counseling functions are so broad and pervasive that no staff members receive the title "counselor." In CETA programs in Iowa run by the governor, for example, traditional counseling roles are assigned to staff members entitled "generalists."

The counseling role is naturally limited by the funding formula and the basic mission of the CETA program. Successful unsubsidized job placement in the private sector is the only criterion for funding in most cases. The CETA prime sponsor or subcontracting agency must successfully place at least 65 percent of its participants if the flow of funds from the Department of Labor is to continue. This formula follows from CETA's mission, described by a Government Accounting Office report of 1978 as an effort "to establish a flexible and decentralized system of federal, state, and local programs for job training and employment opportunities for economically disadvantaged, unemployed, and underemployed persons, and to assure that these services lead to maximal opportunities and enhance self-sufficiency for participants."[6]

Unfortunately, there is sometimes a contradiction between maximizing placements and enhancing "self-sufficiency for participants." The common complaint of counselors and other staff is that counselors are given so many functions that they have little time to see that placements are appropriate to the individual's career plan and personal makeup. The counseling is most often crisis intervention—helping to solve a problem well after it has begun—rather than a developmental approach to the personal growth of the counselee. Counseling sessions rarely offer help in coping with the expectations of employers, making the transition from training with peers to workplaces, understanding the middle-class work ethic and its possible conflict with the counselee's values, handling the stresses resulting from cultural differences and personal conflicts, and examining personal problems—frequently the main reason for dropping out of the training program or the first job. The General Accounting Office study was critical of the failure of CETA programs to provide this form of counseling, noting that "many participants who failed to complete training or obtain jobs might have been helped in some way. More intensive counseling or referring the participant to other agencies for supportive services could have resolved some problems."[7]

The Labor Department has not attempted to provide standards for counselor performance or training assistance to improve that performance. In fact, there are no specialists in counseling in the Employment and Training Administration offices concerned with CETA prime sponsors. "We are all generalists," said one staff member. While some prime sponsors provide in-service training, many are apparently too pressured by the flow of trainees to take time to organize and conduct training. Training expenses must compete with other administrative costs. Many counselors have no specialized training in counseling, having gained experience in a variety of federal employment manpower and social service programs. Those who do have M.A.'s in counseling have been through graduate programs directed either to the school or clinical setting, with little attention to the employment situation.

What support, then, can an adult worker seeking improvement receive from the linkages provided by the CETA program? First, the worker must be eligible for CETA, which means meeting a needs test of income or employment. A person who wishes help in examining completely and thoroughly the personal factors bearing on planning for education and work cannot expect much assistance from a CETA counselor, and a referral to the Employment Service would not greatly increase the chances of satisfaction in this area. The pressure on CETA, as on ES, will be to make an early placement in a training program or a job. Opportunities for sustained contact through a number of counseling sessions with one person are not great in most CETA programs, except with trainers during the actual training.

Exceptions, however, are people who work for Public Service Employment (PSE) under the CETA program. Some of them may benefit from the new requirement that PSE employees be provided with career and employment counseling for a number of months before culminating their assignment and again facing the job market.[8]

Educational Brokering Services

In the 1970s, a new package of linking services for searching adults was developed and delivered in novel ways and settings. Brought together in a single service were six key educational support functions traditionally offered in isolation from one another, if at all: (1) outreach to people not benefiting from educational opportunities; (2) delivery of educational and occupational information; (3) assessment of academic and occupational skills and preferences; (4) counseling on formation of educational and occupational plans; (5) referrals to both educational and social service resources; (6) advocacy for individuals and groups with institutions and agencies that erect barriers to adult learning.

These services were started in community organizations that prided themselves on being free of any institutional self-interest, impartial about the learning decisions clients made, and centered on the needs of clients. Some agencies, such as the Regional Learning Service of Central New York in Syracuse, were designed and created exclusively to be a neutral base for the provision of comprehensive services for would-be adult learners. Some long-established, multipurpose community agencies, such as libraries and YWCAs in a number of cities, added to their programs the new package of adult learner services. In the second half of the 1970s, a number of universities and community colleges, such as Rockland Community College in New York, challenged the charges that they only counseled adults as part of their recruitment efforts. They provided examples of their impartial counseling services, often located off campus in a store-front or community center.

These information and counseling programs for adults came to be known generically as educational brokering services. The name was inspired by their role as intermediaries striving to make a mutually satisfactory match between learners and any of the diverse learning resources in a community. They do not offer courses or credits, nor do they administer examinations and award degrees. They certainly do not recruit or persuade for a given university or college. What they do is to facilitate self-directed planning, decision-making, and action by people who wish to change their lives through additional training or educational activities. They now have a national network headed by the National Center for Educational Brokering (NCEB), a division of the National Institute for Work and Learning (formerly, the National Manpower Institute).[9]

By the end of 1978, the NCEB had identified 302 information and counseling programs which met its criteria for educational brokering services. These criteria stress, first of all, that the information base of the service be truly comprehensive, containing data on educational offerings not at one college, but at all the educational institutions in the community as well as proprietary schools and community agencies. Second, the service must be open to the public, or major segments of the out-of-school public, and be under no pressure to refer clients to a particular institution. Third, the services must be concerned not primarily with job placement, but mainly with helping clients discover their own preferences, competencies, opportunities, and aims for action at the workplace and in the rest of their lives. Because of these criteria, the CETA prime sponsors and the Employment Service offices, with their stress on immediate job placement, are not included in the NCEB listing.

The more than 300 brokering services listed are very similar in the functions they perform; at the same time, they are very different in administrative setting. Approximately 130 of the brokering programs are conducted by independent community agencies such as YMCAs and YWCAs, libraries, the League of United Latin American Citizens, Jewish social services, native

American organizations, and others. Of these, 47 agencies, such as OPTIONS, Inc., in Columbus, Ohio, and WINNERS in Boston, Massachusetts, had been incorporated for the exclusive purpose of providing counseling and information. In addition, there are over 100 individual colleges and universities and 35 consortia of institutions that meet the NCEB criteria of objectivity in their provision of educational information and counseling. Most of these institutions had received grants from the federal government under the TRIO Program of support and outreach services to disadvantaged prospective students. The government regulations require that services be available to nonstudents and that referrals of them be made to all available educational institutions. These 300 programs are offering services at 433 local counseling sites.

The clients of the brokering-type programs in 1978 numbered about 900,-000. They came from all positions on the socioeconomic scale. Some services, especially women's centers, dealt largely with middle-class people. Others, especially the TRIO Programs, focused on economically and socially disadvantaged people under 30. What has been widely observed is that workers on hourly wages have not in large numbers availed themselves of these community counseling services and that there have been no special efforts to reach them. Women in low-paid salaried positions are among the clientele of brokering services, but only a small percentage of clerical and service workers make use of them.

The libraries have made an important start in supporting adult learners, but they represent a relatively undeveloped potential as sites for educational information and advisement centers. New York State, for example, has 45 Job Information Centers located in libraries and run in cooperation with public and private employment and education agencies. In 1979, the State Education Department made six grants to test the potential of libraries as focal points for educational information services in the community.[10]

A number of brokering agencies have made a concentrated effort to market their services with employers in the public and private sectors. Some have been successful in developing a series of educational and occupational planning workshops sponsored usually by management and conducted on site. The agencies have also recruited counseling staff members from the ranks of the workforce. Still, the percentage of clientele in low-paid occupations is not commensurate with their role in the labor force and the country.

An important impetus to educational brokering has been the Education Information Act Centers program, included in the 1976 amendments to the Higher Education Act. This legislation authorizes grants to states (when they submit plans and get them approved) for the purpose of developing and extending guidance, referral, and information services for all residents. By this Act, therefore, public policy has recognized the need to provide such information to adults who might want to resume schooling.

While the policy is clear, the appropriations are relatively small, and the growth of actual services slight compared to the size of the adult population. In fiscal year 1978, $2 million was distributed to 44 states, with each one getting an average of $35,000. In the following two years, the appropriation rose to $3 million, with 48 states and 5 territories participating. This funding has enabled each state to designate an Education Information Centers (EIC) Coordinator and to survey state counseling needs. Information hotlines have been established in a number of states and many have published directories. But this federal aid has been too small to get additional counseling services installed at the local level or to support the expansion of existing brokering programs. There are 2,800 local Employment Service offices operating with public funds to match people and jobs; in comparison, the effort to match adults and educational opportunities is only in a start-up phase.

Linking Services for Women

The fastest-growing sector of educational brokering programs is targeted to the particular needs of adult women. Women make up approximately two-thirds of the clients at adult counseling services that handle both men and women. In addition, there are a number of specialized services for women situated in two main settings: (1) college and university women's centers and (2) community-based women's services. Some of these programs are specifically for displaced homemakers.

College and university women's centers are generally located in the counseling and placement office, the extension division, or the continuing education program. They range in purpose from thinly veiled recruiting ploys to objective community services making referrals to an entire range of educational opportunities in the area. There is usually a strong emphasis on building self-esteem through individual counseling and group experiences. There is also a good deal of career exploration and planning provided. In many cases there is not a very strong information base on other training and educational opportunities outside the institution hosting the service. Group counseling is often provided in the form of a course for credits. One of the earliest programs of this sort is the George Washington University Continuing Education for Women Program, which offers a semester-long course designed for well-educated and unemployed women. Such college programs in the course format tend to attract middle-class women from professional and managerial households. The centers are frequently staffed by graduate students in counseling programs supervised by a credentialed and experienced counselor.

Community-based women's programs are found in mainline organizations such as the YWCAs and in independent organizations created for the purpose of providing mutual assistance among women. One of the first and most durable of the independent community agencies is Wider Opportunities for Women in Washington, D.C., which was founded in 1965 as a small voluntary effort located in Washington's downtown YWCA. It was initially conceived as a clearinghouse of information on part-time work and study opportunities primarily for educated women. Once staffed by volunteers, it now has a paid staff of 25 persons working in a variety of self-supporting and grant-supported programs with more than 10,000 women clients in the first twelve years of operation. The initial clients were largely middle-class, educated women who helped each other reenter the labor force and find the training needed to do so. Peer counseling and self-help are still emphasized, but the basic job advisory and referral service now costs $40, including two months' use of the Center, workshops, and library resources, as well as referrals. Thus, it now is largely self-supporting. Other programs for low-income and unskilled women are funded by the D.C. Manpower Administration and private foundations. They include not only counseling, but training in paraprofessional work and work experience as a rehabilitation program for women offenders.

The total number of such community-based and college-based women's services is not known. Wider Opportunites for Women published a Directory in 1979 that included over 200 centers. The Catalyst organization has over 150 centers in its network, inclusion in which requires one credentialed counselor on the staff and a clientele at least 60 percent female. New nonprofit and for-profit women's services are being created each year. While they tend to emphasize guidance in the labor market, they usually can make referrals to training and educational opportunities as well. Some of them give the greatest emphasis to actual job placement while others, especially those in universities and colleges, take the longer career- and life-planning approach. Many are free, but most charge fees for workshops, courses, and vocational assessment and testing.

Many displaced homemakers programs also sprang into operation in 1978 and 1979. Two pioneering centers are in Oakland, California and Baltimore. The latter was established in 1976 by an independent agency, New Directions for Women, founded four years earlier as a clearinghouse for women on educational, volunteer, and employment opportunities. This model service hosted a national conference in October 1978, which resulted in the establishment of the Displaced Homemakers Network. It now lists in its directory over 100 programs, centers, and projects. Public funding for services to displaced homemakers is more ample than for any other adult population group. Twenty-five states have passed measures to provide assistance to displaced homemakers in preparing for and finding paid jobs. Grants are authorized by such state departments as social services, labor, human resources, health, and welfare to new and traditional community agencies and colleges.

At the federal level, the 1978 amendments to the Comprehensive Employment and Training Act in Title III provided for special services to a series of population groups, including displaced homemakers—defined legally as persons who have not worked in the labor force "for a substantial number of years," but who have provided unpaid services in the home and have been dependent on some form of public assistance or upon the income of another family member which is no longer available or who are receiving public assistance through aid to dependent children, especially when such aid is soon to be terminated, and who, finally, are "unemployed, or underemployed, and are experiencing difficulty in obtaining or upgrading employment." Five million dollars in CETA funds were allocated in the first and second years to support such programs.

The women served by displaced homemakers programs are, on the average, older than the clients of educational brokering services have been. They cluster in the 45- to 55-year age group. To be eligible they must be in immediate need of a job or income. Therefore, the first emphasis in services is upon job placement. Career counseling, personal awareness, and confidence building are also usually included. Some programs continue support after job placements are made and assist women to develop and undertake long-term career planning, including training and education. Generally, however, the emphasis is not on referring women to educational opportunities, at least in the short range. It is estimated that, in 1980, there were between 4 and 6 million people in the country who qualify under the legal definition of displaced homemakers.

Management and Labor

As educational opportunities for working people grow, particularly through the growth of tuition-aid plans, some isolated experiments in providing educational information and advisement at the workplace are beginning. The service is provided by management or unions or, in a few cases, is jointly sponsored by both parties. Educational brokering at the workplace has the potential of playing a very significant role in assisting adults to make educational and occupational choices.

In some firms liberal tuition-aid plans are available and management feels a real interest in getting workers to take advantage of these benefits. For example, employees at Polaroid know where to go in the firm to get substantial help with their educational needs and plans. More of what is known about employer-based educational advisement services is provided in Chapter 10.

While still in the minority, more and more industry tuition-aid plans are the result of collective bargaining agreements. Finally, some education and training benefits are offered unilaterally through unions. These efforts are explored in both Chapter 7 and Chapter 10. There is strong interest in some unions in expanding these services. For example, they are now offered extensively by District 37 of AFSCME in New York City, and the International Ladies Garment Workers Union has recently created such services in their union on a pilot basis on both the East and West Coasts.

Recommendations for Better Connections

While the adaptation and spread of support services tailored to adult needs have been impressive, it is striking that fewer than one million Americans out of school in 1978 received such services. It is hard to see how the adult and worker learning enterprise can be advanced very much further without more adequate arrangements for matching learning seekers and learning opportunities. And if we are to move forward on the learning front, the provision of adequate information and advice may be the cheapest way to get the desired participation from those groups that have had the least connection in the past with the learning system: minorities, lower-income families, and people without high school educations.

We do not, at this point in our history, argue for a wholly government-financed counterpart of the 30,000-employee public Employment Service. There is great diversity in the present system of adult learning, and we see no reason that the provision of educational information and advisement services should not also move forward in different ways in different communities and from a variety of institutional bases. Middle-class, college-trained women may be comfortable with the new women's centers on college campuses, blue- and pink-collar workers may opt for some initial help at the workplace or union hall, and low-income families may place most trust in a neighborhood association. Maybe out of diverse practice only one or two or three approaches will eventually win out in the marketplace, but this may be a suitable method for determining what best meets the needs of people. In the 1980s, the best strategy would seem to be one of encouragement on a variety of fronts, of getting a set of services into place that have some hopes of engaging the full spectrum of adults who may want to pursue learning on an organized basis. Later, there will be time for consolidation and rationalization.

We offer the following principles and practices as suggestions for policies to better meet adult learner needs in making the right connection.

Shared Responsibility

It is important that all participants in the adult learning community recognize their responsibilities for getting their wares before all the people who may want to examine them. Government has an important role, but it would be premature to say that information services should be the primary responsibility of the federal government through turning the Education Information Center Act into a half-billion-dollar appropriation. Nor should this effort be solely the state governments' responsibility. There is a role for community initiative and variation here. Also, responsibility extends far beyond government to educational providers at every level in the system. There is in addition a proper responsibility on the part of the adult seeking learning opportunity. Effort, time, and a moderate financial investment are not too much to expect from those who will benefit most from educational resources—the adult learners themselves.

Improved Educational Information Centers Program

The Congress created in 1976 (in Section 418 of the Higher Education Act) a useful mechanism for increasing the role of state government in supporting information and counseling services for people who have left school. The federal contribution to the Educational Information Centers program has been and ought to be modest. The appropriations should be set at a level sufficient to move toward implementation at the local level, rather than just to provide a staff position or two in the state capitals. The program will have better leverage per federal dollar if, as proposed by the House of Representatives in 1979, it is combined with federal grant programs to states for postsecondary planning and continuing education.

It is also recommended that the Education Information Centers (EICs) advocate on behalf of local information providers and counselors. With state and federal sources of funding, the EIC director is in a good position to convene all state program officers with responsibilities bearing on information and counseling delivery and to encourage their sharing of resources to the benefit of local intermediaries.

Information and Advisement Cost Sharing

There remains a need for more public support for linking mechanisms if educational access is to be equitable in practice. Until the need emerges for more standardized and centralized approaches, there is, we believe, a valid principle from which a diverse set of services could grow, particularly with respect to learning opportunities supported by the government. That principle is that, whenever governments appropriate money actually to provide education and training opportunity, those same appropriations and authorizing statutes should set aside an appropriate portion of the total to support impartial educational information and advisement services. Some discussion and trial and error would establish what proportion of the total that ought to be. What this principle says is that the creation of public education and training opportunities carries with it a responsibility to facilitate access to those opportunities. Such a policy would create a fund for educational information and advisement activities that would grow as public funding of the opportunities themselves grows, and would provide at least minimal assurance that all groups in the population have a chance to take advantage of available opportunities. There is precedence for this approach in the veterans programs that provide not only tuition and living aid to veterans, but also money for counseling services to help veterans use their benefits well.

The contribution of federal education and training programs to the pool of funds that support the information and advisement functions would give programs some voice in shaping policies on the operation of such services. There would be some assurance that if such services were not providing information about, say, opportunities for adults in secondary school vocational programs, there would be oversight from the administrators of the Federal Vocational Education Act to get such defects remedied.

To carry out such a funding arrangement, there would have to be, as far as federally funded programs are concerned, a counterpart of the new National Occupational Information Coordinating Committee (NOICC). A national committee would coordinate the development of education information, brokering, and advisement services for adults seeking organized learning opportunities. EIC Coordinators and their advisory boards, already in place at the state level, would link the national committee with local services. This goes beyond the present role of NOICC, particularly since there are other objectives of adult learning besides occupational preparation. There is, however, a close relationship between the two functions. We would hope that such an effort would also have strong private sector participation and not be solely a government operation.

Educational Advisement Capability in CETA and the U.S. Employment Service

There is a close connection between agencies that help people get jobs by providing occupational counseling and those that primarily help adults formulate educational plans. The connection is that, on the employment side, a lot of career objectives cannot be reached without further education and training. On the education side, a lot of people have a career objective in mind to which educational plans must be related. Therefore, job placement and counseling agencies could be a lot more help to their clients if they were well informed about the whole structure of education and training in the community or worked very closely with a good community-based educational brokering agency.

To improve the ability of the USES and its 2,800 state-run local offices to match job/career objectives with educational objectives for clients, we recommend that USES take the lead in efforts to better equip local offices with this capability. This means perhaps an enlarged concept of the assignment for some ES counselors; more adequate time for counseling where career/educational planning is involved, rather than just quick job placement; and agreements made for cross-referral between local educational brokering agencies and local ES offices.

In the case of programs under CETA, there is the possibility that through contracts with local brokering agencies, clients who seek employment but need further education and training could be enrolled in many regular courses offered by community institutions. This would broaden the reach of CETA beyond those classes and programs established wholly to serve a disadvantaged clientele. To the extent that the purchase of slots for individuals in ongoing programs could be expanded, there would be less of the economic segregation which now often occurs in educational and training settings.

The central point is that, between USES and CETA, there are now several thousand public employment services offices. If their present purpose were slightly enlarged, and if they worked closely with their educational information counterparts, services could be expanded at a relatively low cost. This works two ways, of course. Any agency that is doing educational counseling for adults isn't doing its job unless it, first, becomes knowledgeable about the relationship of education and training to careers and jobs and, second, tries to establish an effective working relationship with job placement agencies in order to tap into sources of good occupational information.

Educational Brokering at the Workplace

It is recommended that public and private sector *employers* adopt a policy that information and guidance for educational decision-making deserves to be considered on a par with the provision of training and the support of education. Such a general policy could be carried out in a number of ways, including the following:

1. Employers could utilize human development and training budgets to provide educational information and counseling to their employees having the lowest levels of education and income in particular and to all other employees in general. This support service could be provided in at least three ways: (1) the human resources/training department or staff could spend more time publicizing educational opportunities in-

house and in the community and advising people on their use; (2) workers in various offices and shops and at various authority levels could be selected and trained to be learning organizers among their peers; and (3) management could contract with community brokering services to provide information and counseling at the worksite.

2. Employers could authorize the use of up to $100 or $150 of tuition-aid funds for employees who wish to work in a systematic fashion with an educational counselor prior to schooling in order to make a suitable educational plan. We believe this would improve choices made by employees and therefore increase the return on investment for both employers and employees.

3. Office libraries should include in their acquisition list standard educational information resources and should publicize their availability.

It is proposed that *labor unions* train shop stewards, business managers, or other local officials to provide educational information and advice to union members. The individuals selected should have access to workers during the workday at the worksite and be recognized by management as having a legitimate role in meeting with other workers to discuss the quality of worklife, including educational opportunities as one way to enhance that quality.

Improving Displaced Homemakers Programs

It is proposed that, in services to displaced homemakers, greater emphasis be given to a continuing process of personal career and educational planning before, during, and after the job search. While the aim of these programs may be job placement, their public funding should be available for longer-term counseling to ensure that the first placement is not the last, but rather part of a career that will progress over many years.

* * * *

In many areas of life in the United States, we place great value on diversity of opportunities, responsiveness to people's needs, and equality of access to whatever the system offers its citizens. And in the economy itself, we place high value on having many suppliers and on the free movement of workers among producers and sellers. We have always known that a key to making such systems work is the availability of correct and timely information. Consumers must know who sells what and at what price. Workers must know where the job openings are and how to qualify for them. The same is true for adult and worker education and training. Merely building and staffing classrooms and programs, while failing to provide maps for getting to them, will mean empty classrooms. An effective information system and an understanding of how access to learning is obtained are both necessary if the right connection is to be made.

There will be a temptation to press on with bricks and mortar, new curricula, different certifications requirements, and as yet unheard-of programs and degrees, without attending first to fundamentals—the need for a sound information base and help for people in negotiating the system. To do so would be a mistake.

Notes

1   *Job Seeking Methods Used by American Workers,* Washington, D.C.: U.S. Bureau of Labor Statistics, 1975.
2   *The Public Employment Service and Help Wanted Ads: A Bifocal View of the Labor Market,* U.S. Department of Labor, R&D Monograph 59, 1978.
3   General Administration Letter No. 911, September 13, 1965, U.S. Department of Labor.
4   General Administration Letter No. 1447, October 14, 1971, U.S. Department of Labor.
5   Stanford Research Institute, *Effectiveness of Counseling in U.S. Employment Service: A Pilot Study,* August 1977.
6   *Job Training Programs Need More Effective Management,* General Acounting Office Report HRD 7896, July 7, 1978, Washington, D.C., p. 26.
7   General Accounting Office Report HRD 7896, p. 14.
8   The principal source for information used here about the conduct of counseling under CETA is *Interviews and Urban CETA-based Guidance Services,* National Center for Research in Vocational Education, Columbus, Ohio, 1979.
9   James Heffernan, Francis Macy, and Donn Vickers, *Educational Brokering: New Services for Adult Learners,* Syracuse, N.Y.: NCEB, 1976.
10 Norman Kurland,"Growth of Lifelong Learning in New York State," in *Implementing New Education-Work Policies,* ed. Paul E. Barton, San Francisco: Jossey-Bass, 1978.

Chapter 5

The Ordeal
of Change

The employer cannot offer and the worker cannot accept the old relations of protection and dependence: for owing to the modern necessity of the constant movement of labor from place to place and from one employment to another, it has become impossible to form lasting relations, and the essence of the old system lay in the permanency of the workmen's engagements.

Arnold Toynbee, *The Industrial Revolution,* 1884

We can never be really prepared for that which is wholly new. We have to adjust ourselves, and every radical adjustment is a crisis in self-esteem: we undergo a test, we have to prove ourselves.

Eric Hoffer, *The Ordeal of Change,* 1952

Changing occupations is an ordeal braved by a significant number of Americans each year. Steadily employed workers suddenly find themselves torn from the security and perhaps the satisfaction of their jobs by economic forces far beyond their control: a decline in automobile sales, an import from Europe, a new technological process. Women who have worked as mothers and home-makers need or want a new career. Older workers, inner-city residents—the ordeal of occupational change is familiar to many. Fast on its heels, the worker often suffers the painful realization that he/she has neither the skills to move into a new occupation nor access to training to learn new skills.

This chapter proposes a public response of occupational adjustment assistance for men and women in the midst of employment transitions which they cannot negotiate without improved or additional skills. The history of occupational readjustment policy in the United States is explored, for the new program of occupational assistance proposed here represents, in some sense, a

73

natural evolution of this earlier policy and the essential principles informing its development. But this recommendation is also derived from a careful consideration of just who suffers from occupational dislocation, and what the effect of this ordeal is upon the economic system and social fabric of which each individual is a part.

Worker Dislocation

The number of Americans changing or contemplating changing their workplace is staggering. The statistics confirm a trend obvious to workers, their friends, families, and neighbors:

- One study found 36 percent of the adult working population either in a work transition or anticipating one.[1]

- Within a single year, 8.3 million men and 6.9 million women changed their occupation.[2]

- Within a single month, 3.3 million employed people were looking for new jobs.[3]

- One comparison study over a decade, by the Bureau of Labor Statistics, discovered that, except for women over 55 years of age, whose job tenure had increased, the average time a worker stays in one job has decreased.[4]

- Depending on whether the business cycle is on the up- or downswing, from 15 to 20 million workers experience unemployment at some time during the year.[5]

Sailing in the waters of the economic system offers good speed to many, the freedom to choose and pursue a new direction to the majority, and the prospect of being blown far off course by strong winds of change for a smaller but significant number.

The American free enterprise economy offers workers the widest range of work options and the highest standard of living in history. It also demands that its workers adapt to perpetual economic change. That the American working population has proved willing to adapt is itself a major element in the nation's economic achievements. But this is not to say that changing jobs, employers, residences, or careers is easy for most. A few years ago, when a psychologist developed a scale to measure emotional trauma, changing jobs tied divorce for first place.

Anyone who remembers the first week on a new job also remembers the strain, even when the change was desired, planned, and ultimately successful.

Fortunately, most job changes become success stories. Much of the drive behind this most successful of modern economies lies in the often-heard phrase, "I was seeking a new challenge." Work is a vital element of life—the means by which we acquire the material necessities. Work also establishes the identities of most men and more and more women. When who we are is linked to what we do, changing jobs, occupations, and careers is bound to create anxiety.

A substantial proportion of workers have skills that remain in demand. They move from firm to firm and place to place according to what seems best for wage and career advancement. Plumbers, aircraft mechanics, and lawyers come to mind. Their life adjustments are more in the mode of Gail Sheehy's *Passages* than of John Steinbeck's *Grapes of Wrath.*

The tens of millions who operate the machines and production lines of the Industrial Revolution's high technology phase sustain reasonably stable worklives if situated within expanding industries and metropolitan areas with a diversified economic base. Their highly specialized jobs constitute a significant proportion of the 23,000 official job titles contained in the federal government's *Dictionary of Occupational Titles.* Workers move from job to job, hearing about opportunities by word of mouth. Savings and unemployment insurance carry them through brief periods of unemployment with relatively little effect on their living standards. These workers in the heart of the industrial economy have what Peter Doeringer and Michael Piore describe as "primary" jobs in the "internal labor market," in which hiring for higher-paying jobs is from within, unions provide protection, fringe benefits are an ever larger proportion of total pay, and a wide variety of skills can be acquired in the firm and on the job.

But there is yet another area of the economy, primarily in the service sector but including some manufacturing, in which there is a low-wage labor surplus. Job attachment is tenuous, fringe benefits low, turnover high, and little training necessary. Many women are in this "secondary labor market," as are many of the minority populations in the inner cities and residents of rural areas. Unemployment is frequent. Although sufficient jobs in the primary labor market often exist, getting one is not so easy, particularly without skills or education.

Yet another growing sector of the workforce is making perhaps the most difficult career change of all: women who have cared for families full-time are now ready for paying jobs. Already working more hours than most men in the endless tasks of the household, women commencing a job search are nevertheless counted as "unemployed" in the official government statistics. The redirection of skills required is substantial, particularly if a woman is to land one of the better jobs in the primary labor market.

Adjustment to Change

The intent here is not to tell a tale of woe. Even when workers are separated from their jobs involuntarily, statistics show that the great majority make new connections within the existing system, relying on informal sources of information including contacts with friends and relatives. Only a small percentage find new jobs through public employment services, even though many register with such services when drawing Unemployment Insurance. Most find new jobs requiring existing skills in lines of work sufficiently similar so that new skills needed can be picked up on the job. Even when occupations are changed completely, most enter fields where employers expect to provide the entry training. This latter route is not open, of course, to professional, technical, or licensed occupations for which academic credentials or standardized tests are required.

To say that these transitions are relatively painless for many is a long way from saying they are so for most. Many workers do not make the transition easily or quickly, if at all. For them, a combination of individual circumstances and local economic conditions blocks a smooth transition; either retraining or educational certification for new jobs is required. Just the prospect of being on the street can send workers into a panic, as happened to Duane Paddleford, age 44, when Baker Plant closed: "You won't believe this—a couple of months after we first heard that the company was thinking about closing us down, my hair began to fall out. Overnight like . . . the doctors said it must have been nerves, so I guess I was pretty worried."[6] A job vanishing out from under you is serious business, even if you eventually land on your feet.

Although the statistics, other than providing a simple count of regular unemployment, don't permit precise analysis of the problem's extent, many workers, perhaps tens of thousands each year, do not land on their feet. They exhaust the financial back-up systems of Unemployment Insurance and personal savings and either recede into the shadows or struggle along on the fringes of the employment world. Workers who need help are to be found among:

- housewives making the change from career motherhood to career something else;
- workers displaced by technology, especially those over forty or in communities with limited opportunities;
- workers abandoned as an industry moves to another part of the country;
- workers trapped in increasingly jobless inner cities;
- workers whose manufacturer employers are put out of business;

- workers trapped in jobs far below their potential and unable to advance with existing skills; and

- older workers almost anywhere.

There are elements of federal education and training policy in the United States which have a direct bearing on the situation of these workers. An examination of this policy's evolution and these elements will lead us to a recommendation for future directions.

Origins of Policy

The history of training and education directed to adult work transitions in the United States begins with the history of worklife education and training itself. This history is marked by extremes: tremedous leaps forward and long periods of stagnation, major policy advances followed by retreats, and sophisticated approaches to some needs while others are hardly recognized.

The origins of a worklife training policy are commonly traced to the 1860s, when, for the first time, fewer people were working in agriculture than elsewhere. The Morrill Act of 1862 responded to the emerging belief that the new industrialism's need for professional and technical training was not being met by either the one-room schoolhouse or the university. The land grants provided by the Act created colleges for "such branches of learning as are related to agriculture and the mechanical arts."

The growing public education system emphasized general rather than vocational education, and the idea that elementary schools could relieve industry of the burden of technical training was rejected by employers and educators alike. While secondary education was to remain comprehensive, the Smith-Hughes Act of 1917, by creating a system of vocational education, assured that some proportion of youth would have the option of learning an employment skill. This Act and its subsequent amendments, occasionally complemented by other public policy developments, have remained the cornerstone of public policy on occupation-specific worklife education. The comprehensive character of public education in the United States was in contrast to the systems of other industrial countries, which channeled youth at an early age toward apprenticeship or work.

The 1930s witnessed an overall loss of workforce skills as much of the population was idled, cut off from employment where skills are most often developed and maintained. Depression policy concentrated on job creation and income security rather than on worker education and training, although such programs as the Civilian Conservation Corps and the National Youth Administration did contribute to youth development.

As World War II absorbed the large pool of human resources, industry was generally found capable of providing necessary training. However, shortages of particular skills necessitated the infusion of public money. The Vocational Education for National Defense Act added $80 million to the normal $15 million outlay for vocational education. In all, institutional training reached more than 7 million prospective war production workers under the Vocational Education for National Defense program.[7] This was the first really large-scale attempt to match adult workers to available jobs through skills training.

The next step, to smooth the transition of veterans from World War II to civilian worklife, proceeded on the unquestioned assumption that education and training provided to the former GI would find application in the postwar economy. Whatever else the GI Bill (the Servicemen's Readjustment Act of 1944) was, it was a huge investment in facilitating occupational change. By 1956, 7.5 million veterans had enrolled at a total cost of $13 billion. The combination of unmet demands for civilian goods, savings accumulated during the war, and the federal government's assumption of responsibility for economic stability under the Employment Act of 1946, resulted in a long period of economic growth punctuated until 1958 by only mild recessions. The GI Bill graduates were readily absorbed into this thriving economy.

The Retraining Initiatives of the 1960s

It did not go unnoticed, however, particularly by Senator Paul Douglas, that postwar growth was uneven. Amidst general affluence, there were "depressed areas." After two vetoes by President Eisenhower, Senator Douglas's Area Redevelopment Act (ARA) was signed into law in 1961 by President Kennedy, who had seen depressed-area poverty firsthand during his primary campaign in West Virginia. The ARA included a program of "retraining" for workers, which by 1964 had enrolled about 39,000 unemployed in 900 projects covering 200 occupations. If the Morrill Act of 1862 marked the beginning of worklife education and training public policy, the ARA is the most direct antecedent of current public programs that ease the employment adjustments of adults by paying them stipends while they learn.

In fact, the years 1961 and 1962 saw a burst of public policy initiatives concerning employment adjustment. A pattern was set, which has endured with variations ever since, of collaborative efforts between the manpower (or labor-market) agencies and the state vocational education systems. The broadest such effort, which led directly to the present CETA, was the Manpower Development and Training Act of 1962. A second development, likely to have greater impact in the future than it has had to date, is the Worker Adjustment Assistance Program authorized by the Trade Expansion Act of 1962.

Under the Manpower Development and Training Act (MDTA), workers dislocated from their jobs were retrained for other jobs, either in the classroom, through joint Employment Service and vocational education system collaboration, or on the job by reimbursing expenses incurred by employers. The Department of Labor administered the act, but transferred money for classroom training to the Department of Health, Education, and Welfare, which in turn disbursed funds to the vocational education agencies. Workers who became unemployed qualified for MDTA training regardless of why their previous jobs were lost. However, "the primary concern at that time was to retrain persons who were expected to be displaced by automation and technological change and to help them rebuild their skills to meet the occupational needs of the labor market."[8]

In the early 1960s, technological change seemed rampant to many observers, and the facts supported the assertion that the annual rate of productivity was exceeding its recent trend lines. Workers' fears of being idled by technology were undoubtedly reinforced by the high unemployment level at the outset of the Kennedy Administration—a result of the moderately severe recession which followed on the heels of a sluggish recovery from the 1958–59 recession. Recovery from the recession was still incomplete as new training legislation was under consideration by Congress early in 1962.

The MDTA was passed by Congress with overwhelming bipartisan support in March 1962; to emphasize its importance to the Kennedy Administration, the White House asked the Bureau of the Budget (now the Office of Management and Budget, or OMB) to expedite staff work so that the bill could be signed immediately. It was, and the President's signing statement began:

> The Manpower Development and Training bill . . . is perhaps the most significant legislation in the area of employment since the historic Employment Act of 1946.
> . . . The new training program will give real meaning to that Act by making possible the training of the hundreds of thousands of workers who are denied employment because they do not possess the skills required by our constantly changing economy.

In closing, the President sounded a theme familiar to Americans since his assumption of the Presidency: "The success in fulfilling our responsibilities to the world rests upon the success of our efforts to maintain a strong and flexible economy at home."

The purpose of the MDTA were:

- to provide a means of helping workers adjust to job loss inherent in the workings of a free and changing economy

- to keep workers from sinking into poverty that could result from failure to adjust

- to meet the real skill needs of industry

- to be the first real marriage (even if by shotgun) of the labor-market authorities (the Department of Labor and the state Employment Service system) and the education authorities (the Department of Health, Education, and Welfare and the state and local vocational education system)

- to require a joint government and industry effort to administer an on-the-job training program for the unemployed

- to link education/training policy with economic policy, as debate raged in the early 1960s between structuralists, who thought workforce skills did not match the skill requirements of available jobs, and the aggregate demand theorists, who thought higher unemployment was due to insufficient aggregate demand.

Role of the Structuralist–Aggregate Demand Debate

The debate between the aggregate demand school and the structuralist school had the unfortunate effect of throwing retraining and other approaches to redress structural imbalances into competition with a tax cut as a means of dealing with the unemployment that remained after each post–World War II recession. This opposition arose partly because Keynesian economics would not have a chance to affect the economy until the big tax cut of 1964, and because economists advocating aggregate approaches were so committed to the battle to achieve a tax cut that they resisted any diversion of attention to training approaches.

Away from the heat of debate over immediate priorities, the structuralists, who see labor-market imbalances, and the economists, who deal chiefly in fiscal and monetary policy, basically realized that the two policy approaches were complementary rather than competitive. The debate between the two still persists in certain instances, even though a sensible view of their fundamental compatibility was stated as early as 1964 by Paul Samuelson, a widely respected economist who was not in the government at that time:

> There is no hard and fast line between structural and non-structural unemployment. The alleged hard core of the structurally unemployed is in fact made of ice and not iron. The core of ice can be melted over a period of time by adequate effective demand, or it can be solidified from inadequate overall demand. Specific measures for enhancing labor mobility, for retraining and relocating people, for improving employment exchanges, and the organization of the labor market will by themselves help melt the core of structural unemployment, but they are most

needed and work most effectively when aggregate demand measures are being vigorously promulgated.[9]

What is instructive about this debate during the early 1960s is the widespread recognition that adequately equipping workers with the skills to cope with economic change is as important for national economic growth and well-being as it is for displaced workers. Worker retraining policy has both a systems and an individual aspect, in which both public and private interests have a stake.

While fears of technological displacement and efforts to treat structural unemployment were the forces which initially shaped public policy on retraining, President Johnson's decision to declare a "war on poverty," a plan conceived in the last days of the Kennedy administration, forcefully affected policy development thereafter.

Retraining Drafted for Poverty War

The "war on poverty," embodied in the Economic Opportunity Act of 1964, was not an income transfer program. Instead, it was based on two operating principles. One was that individuals could become self-supporting through a variety of services, including employment training. The second was a political assumption that "community action" through "maximum feasible representation" of the poor in the development and administration of programs would reduce their powerlessness and poverty.

It quickly became apparent that MDTA training could be used to fight the poverty war. The Office of Economic Opportunity (OEO) searched for programs which should be redirected toward the poor; the Department of Labor began to move program slots to unemployed people who met the income test of the poverty program. According to Charles Stewart, "it took about five years to change the ratio from 1 disadvantaged out of 3 enrollees to 2 out of 3, and more years before reaching and fluctuating around 4 disadvantaged out of 5."[10] While the results vary among age-sex-race groupings and evaluation studies, research using control groups has generally established that the cost-benefit ratio in these programs is favorable.[11] On the other hand, since the retraining element of these programs directed to adults has not grown substantially, while the components for youth have, only limited claims can be made about the dent retraining programs have made in poverty.

As the 1960s progressed, OEO's programs and the Labor Department's training program became intertwined until, at the local level, they were one and the same. As the burden of direct contracting and the weight of a central, federal administration became more oppressive, reform movements began to "decentralize and decategorize" the MDTA programs. The result was the passage in 1974 of the Comprehensive Employment and Training Act (CETA), which absorbed and entirely recast the MDTA programs.

Today, the worker retraining program, begun in 1961 and 1962, is one element of an "employment and training" program administered by mayors and governors with federal money. It is also a means-tested poverty program, more in the shadow of welfare programs than of either Unemployment Insurance or Social Security.

Two other threads running through this cloth are the Work Incentive Program (WIN) and the Worker Adjustment Assistance Program authorized under the Trade Expansion Act, as amended. WIN includes a large training program administered through the public Employment Service and the Social Services Administration for welfare clients, predominantly women. Although under different administration, it resembles CETA training in the basics. Another occupational adjustment program, apparently much less significant than the MDTA, was enacted by Congress in 1962. The Trade Expansion Act of 1962 took a new approach to the harmful effects of imports on American industries. The choice was between raising tariffs or helping threatened businesses and workers adjust to inexorable changes. For displaced workers, the Worker Adjustment Assistance Program was created. Since the early eligibility criteria proved restrictive, there was little activity under this program until after its revision in 1974.

The Worker Adjustment Assistance Program, while to date seldom used except to authorize weekly cash payments to displaced workers, is perhaps the broadest employment and training act written for adult workers. It provides for counseling, retraining, relocation, and placement services. Training can be subsidized for more than a year. However, only 15,537 workers have benefited from the training program since the 1974 amendments, out of a total of 414,379 who have received cash assistance. Even fewer (1,295) have received relocation allowances, an adjustment benefit not available under CETA, although the idea was experimented with during the 1960s. In 1980, the cost of programs under the Trade Expansion Act leaped upward, as imports increased; and in 1981, Reagan moved to reduce benefit levels.

Given the record of almost two decades, what does this experience suggest for the 1980s? Are there four or five evolving principles that might guide these efforts in the near future?

Further Decentralization: Beyond Local Government

The straightest path followed by retraining policy has been toward decentralization. The early contracts and agreements under MDTA were negotiated directly from Department of Labor headquarters. Later, day-to-day administration was the responsibility of that agency's regional offices. But as the 1960s ended, the Labor Department found itself mired in thousands of individual contracts. The Comprehensive Employment and Training Act of 1973 delegated administration to mayors and governors, who were to be "the prime sponsors." While no one could claim outstanding success for this vast and diverse effort, most observers judge decentralization to have been a correct decision.

A major impasse has been the inability of mayors' offices to achieve private sector involvement. The on-the-job training element of CETA, through which employers provide training and are reimbursed, has not advanced as far as it must, although the National Alliance of Business substantially promoted business involvement.

In 1979, the new Title VII of CETA gave legislative sanction to further decentralization. It created the Private Industry Councils, which have a primarily business membership but also representation from unions, educational institutions, and community-based organizations. The Councils act as intermediaries between local prime sponsors and employers, simplifying employer involvement and exercising judgment in shaping training programs purchased with CETA funds. The first full year's appropriation is expected to be $400 million.

Although the chasm between CETA, a public program, and private sector organizations has at least been diagnosed, the steps taken so far to narrow it are tentative and insufficient. The chasm is too wide to cross with bridgeheads pushed outward only from the public side. The training and placement components of CETA and other government-sponsored efforts, at least so far as private sector employment is concerned, cannot progress far without several absolutely essential ingredients:

- Recognition that most training is provided on the job by employers, or jointly by employers and unions;

- Direct involvement of employers in shaping content and skill areas, if they are expected to employ the people trained;

- Union participation in training arrangements in unionized firms and industries;

- Community education institutions capable of providing back-up in basic and occupational skills education;

- A bridging of the gap between employment and educational institutions, which will not be closed solely by closer employer–CETA prime sponsor relationships;

- True participation by employers, which confers responsibility, rather than attempts to make private organizations mere adjuncts of government programs; and

• Sensitivity to client needs and aspirations similar to that developed in community-based organizations.

The recognition that these elements are essential to any effort to move "unemployable" adults into private sector employment leads to the conclusion that decentralization must go further.

Responsibility for the training and basic education component of CETA, and perhaps other programs as well, should devolve upon those with the power to discharge it. This means responsibility must move still further away from government, whether local or national. Instead of "industry" councils, more substantial roles for education, labor, and community-based organizations must be legislated. We must recognize that since these funds are from public treasuries, rather than "private" councils, both private and public involvement are crucial. While joint responsibility for setting policy and objectives is recognized, a clear executive voice to carry out these policies must also be provided.

The recommendation of this analysis is that responsibility for occupational adjustment efforts be given to *public-private collaborative councils,* with full participation of the critical sectors described above, and funding far greater than the $400 million currently earmarked. The boundaries of these councils' discretion would be set by government, at least concerning the disposition of government funds. Each council would arrange to execute its own policies. A public effort to secure a private outcome can only be achieved through a public-private partnership. This could be Phase II in the evolution of Private Industry Councils.

Offense and Defense

What began in 1962 under MDTA as a broad program of occupational readjustment through retraining has dwindled in scope to a means-tested poverty program for only the most disadvantaged. In 1978, William Mirengoff and Lester Rindler summarized the state of CETA this way:

A three-tier system seems to be evolving: (a) employability programs (Title I) for the severely disadvantaged, (b) public service employment for those higher on the socio-economic ladder, and (c) project-type public service employment for the long-term unemployed in families above the poverty level but below the low-income level.[12]

Although public employment opportunities have expanded, the retraining approach has in the meantime narrowed in focus to those with the lowest incomes; the options for dislocated workers have narrowed as well.

The evolution of an occupational retraining program for workers wrenched from their jobs by the vicissitudes of economic change into a program designed to root out poverty is defended on two counts. The first argument is that the poorest people need the program most. The second is that training is a way to remove people from welfare status. These arguments are eminently sound. To the extent that the lack of an occupational skill prevents a person with a poverty-level income from becoming self-supporting through employment, providing such training is sound public policy. It would be unfortunate, however, if the war on poverty simply treated illnesses, rather than tracking down the virus itself. There is no logic to a treatment approach which overlooks the value of prevention.

To attempt to forestall the economic changes which throw some workers out of jobs is neither feasible nor wise. But we can provide adjustment mechanisms for that small percentage of dislocated workers without the resources or the opportunities to adjust unaided. By providing assistance while workers still believe in themselves, before their confidence is eroded by years of failure, we can prevent workers and their families from slipping into poverty and dependency. Where rapid adjustment is possible, dependency status can be avoided and workers will escape the alienation that often occurs among people excluded by the system.

A more broadly based occupational adjustment service would not fight poverty with less vigor than does the present income-tested approach targeted to the poor. The view of poverty embodied in the program created during the 1960s and carried into the present is a static one. It visualizes a fixed population of poor people, who remain in that status until someone lifts them out. What it does not take into account is the fact that any year's poverty statistic is the net result of the families who enter poverty status and those who leave.

The static interpretation has validity. But equally valid are efforts to prevent economic dependency. It is the difference between successful teaching and remedial education, between adequate private pension plans and old age assistance, and between termite inspection and replacing rotted wood. Both approaches to retraining are recommended. Retraining should be provided to people already in poverty according to the income test. But at the same time, occupational adjustment through retraining is essential for workers dislocated from the system. Preventive assistance would signal a return to the broad policy embodied in the Manpower Development and Training Act and in the Worker Adjustment Assistance provisions of the Trade Expansion Act. Since all studies of the costs and benefits of retraining show positive returns to both the individual and the economy, there is no reason to think such efforts represent a net drain on the nation's resources.[13]

This is not a plea to turn back the hands of time. Much of significance has been accomplished since the passage of the MDTA, particularly decentralization. Rather, this is a recommendation to return to the broader purpose the MDTA originally embodied and to adopt simultaneously both remedial and structural or preventive measures. The MDTA advisory committee was chaired by Eli Ginzberg, who reported on President Kennedy's remarks in support of the broad purpose at its first meeting:

> The three groups cited by the President were:
>
> The large number of young people who were leaving school, poorly educated and poorly trained;
>
> Middle-aged people who had the misfortune to lose their jobs and who could not be readily absorbed in the labor market without a booster such as a retraining program; and
>
> Those persons who possessed very real skills, but skills made obsolescent by a technological development.[14]

To these add the women who need training to gain economic parity and the older workers who need second careers rather than retirement, and a broad program of occupational adjustment would result. Its administration would, of course, have to be a joint public-private undertaking, quite different from the classroom approach used almost exclusively in the early years of the MDTA.

Measures of Success

In evaluating occupational retraining programs, it has become standard to measure their success by whether there was a gain in income and a reduction in unemployment. Sometimes the comparison is to the post-training earnings and unemployment, and sometimes the net change from pre- to post-enrollment is compared with a control group not receiving publicly aided training. This measure reflects the prevailing purpose of such training, which is to take the long-term unemployed or people who have not negotiated the employment system and try to qualify them for entry-level jobs with subsistence earnings at least. For this purpose, this measure is appropriate.

However, as the objectives of retraining programs are broadened along the lines recommended in this chapter, the measures of success cannot be so limited. Facilitating occupational adjustment to forced change is not the same thing as giving people sunk in poverty skills with which to get out. A few examples of other possible measures of success will help make the point:

- Has the program prevented those served from sinking into poverty in the first place?

- Did the occupational change sought actually occur or has the trainee simply continued in a previous line of work?

- Was the need for retraining minimized by appropriate use of less expensive measures such as job placement services? Is training going only to those who need it?

- To what degree are there links between public training authorities and private employers to maximize the use of employer facilities for training?

- To what degree do these training programs enlarge the employment beachheads of women and minorities rather than reinforce traditional labor market practices?

- Although present evaluation criteria emphasize income gain, a realistic adjustment assistance program might still be judged successful in the case of a high-wage worker, displaced by technology and retrained for employment with lower earnings, if the alternative were years of unemployment or unskilled labor at even lower wages.

- Any measure of success should include the subjective feelings of the clients about the degree to which they were helped; evaluators' control groups are of little meaning to the persons who need help.

Women's Share

While the proportion of female enrollees in CETA training has grown in recent years, women have yet to achieve a share equal to their proportion in the job market. In CETA Title I training programs (FY 1975), women comprised 56 percent of enrollees in classroom training programs, but only 26 percent of enrollees in On-The-Job (OJT) Training programs. In the successful Job Corps program for the youthful disadvantaged (FY 1977), only 31 percent of enrollees were women, even though women aged 16 to 21 represent 47 percent of the unemployed and the Job Corps' mandated goal was 50 percent female enrollment.[15] Enrollment of women in Public Service Employment programs, designed to provide a transition to regular employment, lags behind their proportion of the eligible population.[16] According to Isabel Sawhill (then Director of the National Commission on Manpower Policy):

> There is evidence that women have been disproportionately concentrated in the least effective programs and that placements of women enrollees via CETA . . . tend to reproduce the patterns of occupational segregation and wage differential found in the regular labor market. For example in FY '76 . . . 99 percent of all placements into craft jobs under CETA were male while 85 percent of all placements into clerical jobs were female.[17]

Even the Work Incentive Program, which presumably focuses its efforts on female heads of households, has underrepresentation of women relative to their proportion in the eligible population. In FY 1976, women accounted for 90 percent of the target population but only 76 percent of the enrollees.[18]

An occupational adjustment program broader than the present CETA training effort would have as a priority facilitating female entry into the workforce. Beyond the entry level, which traps all too many in lower-paying "women's jobs," upgrading programs are needed to guide women out of these jobs and into better ones. Occupational parity for women would be a key objective of an Occupational Adjustment Program.

Full Use of Community Resources

As occupational adjustment assistance is made available to more workers dislocated from previous employment or entering the labor market for the first time as adults, all the community's training resources should be tapped. The original MDTA program is a good model with respect to its broad purposes, but it was too narrowly conceived in its use of training resources. The tendency in MDTA-CETA-type programs has been to rely too heavily on the public classroom.

This is not to say that the public classroom is inappropriate for certain skills and circumstances. In fact, the public vocational education system should be a primary resource for those changing occupations. Skill centers, such as the excellent one in Hamden County, Massachusetts, are models to build on, but not the only answer, even for classroom training. Nor should classroom training be the sole approach to reequipping adults with occupational skills.

The entire postsecondary educational structure should be a source of training, particularly local community colleges and post–high school technical schools. These institutions are increasingly turning their attention to adults. The median age at community colleges is now 27, much higher than at other postsecondary educational institutions. About 49 percent of full-time and 87 percent of part-time students also work either full- or part-time.[19] Although the working age adults these institutions are reaching may be younger, as yet inexperienced with drastic occupational changes, these institutions must become capable of serving older adults as well.

Another rich source of training is the proprietary school, called, in surveys by the National Center for Education Statistics, private "noncollegiate postsecondary schools." In 1978, these schools had 820,000 enrollees. Their public counterparts accounted for another 350,000 enrollees.[20] Retraining authorities could contract with these schools to provide training for persons dislocated from employment or could simply pay the tuition of clients referred to such schools.

For many occupations and circumstances, the best training is provided by the firm; classroom instruction is supplementary, if required at all. The MDTA-CETA system has taken an on-the-job training approach that reimburses employers' training costs for the eligible workers hired. This approach becomes more promising as administration is delegated to the new Private Industry Councils. An expansion of this approach is to contract with firms to provide skill training for workers who may be placed in employment elsewhere. One example is the Bay De Noc Community College in the Upper Peninsula of Michigan, which provides occupational training to the college's students through contracts with local industry.

These are illustrations of how the entire skill training base can aid workers in need of new skills to make a successful job adjustment. New or expanded educational programs are not necessarily the sole successful ingredients of a skill training system.

In creating an Occupational Adjustment Assistance program as proposed here, care must be taken to avoid setting up skill training programs first and then trying to fit workers into them. Rather, individual workers' needs should first be explored and on that basis, appropriate programs developed. Such flexibility can be maintained if the program builds upon the example of counselors for the Vocational Rehabilitation Administration who assess the individual's needs and who order needed assistance, whether that be the purchase of a back brace or the payment of tuition at the community college. A counterpart could be an Occupational Adjustment Counselor, empowered to make decisions, who could avoid the arbitrary decision-making that creates "slots" in training programs without consulting individual workers.

Conclusion

While most workers dislocated from their jobs by economic change are successful in making an occuaptional adjustment on their own, there are those who need new skills and assistance in acquiring them. The need for new skills and for income while learning is shared by the ever-larger number of women changing from career motherhood to career something else.

In the early 1960s, efforts began to facilitate occupational adjustment under the Manpower Development and Training Act, the Area Redevelopment Act, and the Worker Adjustment Assistance Program in the Trade Expansion Act. The programs which have evolved from the MDTA and ARA largely limit training to those below a certain income. Although training is an important element of any effort to reduce poverty, it is at least as important as a means to prevent workers dislocated by economic change from ever sinking into poverty. As we continue with remedial efforts, we should also develop a preventive approach: a broad Occupational Adjustment Assistance Program, available to workers soon after employment ceases, once it is clear that a new skill is necessary to keep a worker from poverty and dependency.

Occupational Adjustment Assistance would necessarily be carried out through a public-private partnership and not through government alone. The new Private Industry Councils are a model which could be followed here, although with greater representation for educational institutions. Most training would be provided by industry, frequently with labor union involvement. All the community's education and training resources, not just the public classroom, would be utilized for displaced workers. The history of what we have done in the past makes a large role for public vocational education and community colleges obvious. Such a program should erode sex stereotyping, not reflect or reinforce it. Rather than repeat past mistakes by creating large programs with preselected training "slots" into which workers are fit, we should assess worker needs and aspirations on an individual basis and purchase appropriate training from the best possible facility for each particular skill.

Occupational change is an ordeal for workers who are dislocated from one job without the skills for another. Both the worker and the system have an interest in using retraining to keep workers within the employment system who cannot make the adjustment on their own. Retraining can serve as a safety net to keep people from falling into poverty, as well as a way to rescue those already poor.

Notes

1 Solomon Arbeiter et al., *Career Transitions: The Demand for Counseling,* Policy Studies in Education, Executive Summary, Vol. 1, New York: College Entrance Examination Board, 1977.
2 James Byrne, *Occupational Mobility of Workers,* Washington, D.C.: Bureau of Labor Statistics, 1975, p. 58.
3 Special Labor Force Report 175, *Job Tenure of Workers,* Washington, D.C.: Bureau of Labor Statistics, 1975.
4 Special Labor Force Report 202, *The Extent of Job Search by Employed Workers,* Washington, D.C.: Bureau of Labor Statistics, 1977.
5 Bureau of Labor Statistics, annual surveys of work experience of the population.
6 Alfred Slote, *Termination: The Closing of Baker Plant,* New York: Bobbs-Merrill, 1969, p. 122.

7 Grant Venn, *Man, Education, and Manpower,* — Press, 1970, p. 151, and W. S. Woytrinsky and Associates, *Employment and Wages in the United States,* 1953, p. 177.

8 William Mirengoff and Lester Rindler, *CETA: Manpower Programs Under Local Control,* National Academy of Sciences, Washington, D.C., 1978, p. 194.

9 Paul Samuelson, *Economics: An Introductory Analysis,* New York: McGraw-Hill, 1964, p. 783.

10 Charles Stewart, *Worklife Education and Training, and The Ordeal of Change,* National Institute for Work and Learning, 1980, p. 21.

11 There is extensive literature reporting these studies. For a summary see Paul E. Barton, "Adult Education, Work, and Economic Development," in *Entitlement Studies,* ed. Norman Kurland, NIE, 1977.

12 Mirengoff and Rindler, p. 219.

13 For a summary of major cost-benefit studies of retraining programs, see Barton, Table 2, p. 160.

14 *Manpower Advice for Government,* National Manpower Advisory Committee Letters, U.S. Department of Labor, 1972.

15 *Employment and Training Report of the President,* 1978, p. 49.

16 Isabel Sawhill, testimony before U.S. Senate Hearing, "In The Coming Decade: American Women and Human Resource Policies and Programs," Washington, D.C.: U.S. Senate Committee on Labor and Human Resources, 1979, Table 1, p. 553.

17 Sawhill, p. 554.

18 Lorraine Underwood, *Women in Federal Manpower Programs,* Washington, D.C.: The Urban Institute, 1978, p. 16.

19 From American Association of Community and Junior Colleges, October, 1979. (Personal communication.)

20 *The Condition of Education,* National Center for Education Statistics, 1979, p. 102.

Chapter 6

Training in Industry: A Private Affair

18th Century

As population increased and towns grew up . . . there appeared a class of free artisans who worked for hire. Apprenticeship came in time to be associated with the master artisans, as a method of recruiting and training the younger generation of craftsmen.

> Bogart and Kemmerer, *Economic History of the American People,* 1942

19th Century

With the rise of the factory in the 19th century, there was no longer the need for as large a proportion of skilled workers in industry as formerly.

> Paul H. Douglas, *American Apprenticeship and Industrial Education,* 1921

20th Century

There was almost a total ignoring of the human element in the entire system.

> John G. Kemeny, Chairman, Investigation of the Three Mile Island Disaster, 1979

An apprentice craftsman in an American colony, an unskilled factory worker in 1890, and a worker in a nuclear plant who knows what the hundreds of gauges are saying would all find their counterparts throughout American industry in 1980. The eras described in the quotations above are all parts of the modern landscape. This is perhaps the largest reason why almost nothing said in general about the character of present-day training within industry applies to any specific plant or industry.

This fact is central to gaining any perspective on the nature of training provided within industry. This merger of different pasts with the present, the unevenness of the availability of facts, and the contradictions apparent in the variety of approaches to training require some tolerance on the part of anyone trying to understand industrial practice.

The making of things before factories were invented required workers such as carpenters, masons, millwrights, and wheelwrights to have highly developed and exacting skills. The period of training was as long as seven years, although even in Colonial times, training was cut short when labor was scarce: "half-trained artisans began to labor as journeymen and sometimes workmanship suffered."[1] The apprenticeship approach, with learning on the job under joint labor-management agreements to train workers broadly skilled in their crafts, is alive and well today.

The introduction of the factory system, perfected by "scientific management" (invented by Frederick Taylor) and the production line, broke down tasks to their smallest components; workers performed ever narrower roles that could be learned in a few days or hours. This goal was embodied in Taylor's caricature of the result of his own work, when he wrote, "One of the very first requirements for a man who is fit to handle pig iron as a regular occupation is that he shall be so stupid and so phlegmatic that he more resembles an ox than any other type."[2]

And while apprentice and operative carry on, the surge of technology and huge investments in complex industrial processes, often guided by computers, have created a new demand for highly skilled workers. The skills required are often complex and are also ever changing. The spotlight has been much more on the miracles of the technology than on the more humdrum matter of the technical training this technology requires. This gap was brought before the public eye in very dramatic fashion when the advanced technology of nuclear energy was found by the Kemeny Commission (investigating the Three Mile Island disaster) to be operated by inadequately trained personnel. When large corporations speak of serious shortages of trained workers, they are usually referring to the people necessary to service high-technology sectors.

With regard to training in the U.S., there has been a reasonably clear demarcation between public concerns and private ones. Whether for a journeyman, factory operative, or technician, the imparting of skills once a worker is hired is a private affair. While the potential worker is in a school system, education or training may be publicly funded wholly or in part. There are, to be sure, areas of overlap in publicly funded programs, such as the on-the-job training of the disadvantaged under CETA. But these overlaps account for an almost insignificant proportion of total training.

But to speak of such a sharp dichotomy between public interest and private interest based wholly on who performs the training and spends the money is to miss the critical importance of performing the training job adequately. The productivity of the American economy is the concern of all citizens, as workers, consumers, and taxpayers. Nevertheless, the *control* of training within industry is wholly a private affair. All observations and recommendations here are based on it remaining so.

This chapter focuses on the character of industrial training, its purpose and its extent. A few observations are distilled on possible future directions; they are intended for consideration primarily by those decision-makers in the private sector who have the responsibility for this future. The chapter will concentrate almost entirely on training required by and provided by the firm; workers' options in tuition-aid programs are explored in Chapter 10. The involvement of unions in training is treated in Chapter 7.

Industry as Instructor

Underlying all training which industry provides is the education and training workers have received before they are hired, in the home and in the school. In earlier times, what was learned in the home was directly relevant to work, either because young people went to work in the family business—farm or corner grocery—or followed in the occupations of their parents. Since this is seldom true today, formal education carries a larger burden than ever.

The employing institutions pick up where educational institutions leave off. But the interrelationships are so close as to make obvious the artificiality of this division of school and work. Ask employers in the United States today about the quality of worklife preparation, and the most ready response is likely to have something to do with the public schools and how they are doing their job.

From the employer's viewpoint, an initial precondition for their own training is an adequate basic education, which they do not expect to be required to provide. And the statistics offer comfort here, for by the mid-1970s, more than four-fifths of all youth in their early twenties had completed four years of high school or more, and more than one-fifth had completed four or more years of college.[3] In terms of years of schooling, the raw material for training is more advanced than ever before, anywhere in the world. And this fact probably has a lot to do with the success employers and unions generally have in teaching job skills in informal settings.

But these statistics on years of school completed mask an underlying problem that is a growing concern to industry—the problem that too many young people are exiting from the schools with inadequate skills in reading, writing, and arithemetic, and that near illiterates are not uncommon among young people owning high school diplomas. While this is not the place to explore this situation, the picture of industrial training would be incomplete without note of it.

The other large component of the preparation for work before employment is the skill training of a vocational and occupational nature which takes place in the nation's secondary and postsecondary schools. The degree to which a worker is adequately prepared for an occupation in school varies greatly; a high school course in data processing is probably only a bare beginning, but a graduate nurse is ready to assume full responsibility the first day on the job. In most cases, the employer will expect to provide at least limited job-specific instruction, and in a high proportion of hirings a good deal more.

While the bulk of job skills in the U.S. are acquired in the firm, the scale of preparation by schools and training institutions detached from private employment is also vast, and should be comprehended as heavily influencing the size of the task left for employers and unions. The most careful and complete inventory of the *completions* (as opposed to initial enrollments) of vocationally oriented education programs has been compiled by Harold Goldstein, former Associate Director of the Bureau of Labor Statistics, and appears in the table below:

Type of Institution	Number	Percentage of youth at appropriate ages
Secondary school vocational curricula	1,378,000	32.5
Postsecondary vocational curricula, non-college, total	885,000	20.9
Public	537,000	12.7
Private	348,000	8.2
Institutions of higher education, total	1,169,000	29.8
Community college occupational curricula	243,000	5.8
4-year college, no graduate or professional degree	551,000	14.0
First professional degrees (health fields, law, theology)	63,000	1.7
Graduate degrees, masters	312,000	8.3
Adult and on-the-job programs, total	984,000	-
Apprenticeship (registered programs)	49,000	1.3

Military training applicable to civilian jobs	475,000	12.6
Adult vocational education	235,000	-
CETA classroom (130,000) and on-the-job (63,000) training	193,000	-
Job Corps	32,000	-

Source: For a fuller description and detailed reference to sources, see Table 1 and Appendix A in Harold Goldstein, *Training Provided by Industry*, Worker Education and Training Policies Product, National Manpower Institute, 1980.

The raw material for entry into industry and further development there is the nearly one-third of 18-year-olds completing secondary vocational education; the approximately 30 percent of applicable age groups (those in the age range for a particular level of education) completing occupational higher education; the 21 percent of applicable age groups completing postsecondary public vocational education and private trade, technical, and business school programs; the large numbers who acquire skills as professionals; and those completing training as adults in adult vocational programs, CETA classrooms, and military training programs applicable to civilian jobs. A much larger share of young people enter work with vocationally oriented education than is generally assumed from looking at vocational education enrollments alone.

Workplace training picks up where schools leave off. General skills are applied to specific jobs, orientation to the firm has to be provided, and remedial programs are instituted to make up for basic skills not gained in school. Employers have become more critical of schools as they find more need for these remedial programs.

This entry of new workers is only a starting point. For the primary job sector of the economy, where pay is good and employment stable, almost all hiring is at the entry level, and the most advanced jobs are filled from within.[4] This means that workers must be exposed to training which upgrades their skills so that they can advance on the skill ladder. The usual mode is through on-the-job instruction, ranging from very informal to highly structured.

This internal labor market is by no means a static one. Where new product lines are introduced, new skills are often required. Where new advanced equipment is introduced, the workers must be retrained to use it or trained for other jobs in the firm. In fact, the adjustments often run both ways: just as the design of new machinery and the industrial process is fitted to the capabilities of the workers, workers are also trained to use the machinery. This two-way adjustment was clearly observed in an in-depth study of twenty manufacturing plants.[5]

While there is the primary impetus of the need of an employer for a particular skill, the role of training in providing access to the better jobs widens the motivations of employers in providing it. In one of the major studies of training, Seymour Lusterman of the Conference Board identifies the desire to assure "occupational vitality—morale, in the sense of commitment to work—particularly among professionals and managers." And a clear opportunity for training and advancement may make a firm's lower-paying jobs attractive to workers willing "to trade lower pay for learning opportunity."[6]

The pressure on firms to provide equal access to jobs for minorities and increasingly for women has put the spotlight more on the kind of training and remedial education that enables firms to accommodate these new workers. Training on this front has been more publicly visible in the last decade as employers have become involved with the National Alliance of Business and CETA programs.

For the most part, however, industry training remains a quiet affair, an integral part of the production of goods and services and so commonplace in industry that it is uncommonly invisible. But when major industrial crises arise, the adequacy of training is no somnolent issue; it can spring before the public in the daily newspaper, as when a training program was established for the operating staff of nuclear electric generating plants after the Three Mile Island near-disaster and when a special training program was created for air maintenance workers after the tragic crash of a DC-10 in 1979.

Uniform Diversity

About the only uniformity that can be found in the industrial training system is the certainty that, whatever the area of inquiry, there will be diversity in industry's theory and practice. The greatest degree of diversity is to be found in the length and difficulty of the training itself; this diversity stems from the three industrial phases commented on at the outset; the crafts period, the factory period, and the high-technology period. Also to be considered are the skills involved in selling goods and performing services.

A very high proportion of jobs in business need either no or very little training. An assembly-line worker may be at full production by the end of the first day; training may be more a matter of getting accustomed to the rhythms required than of acquiring skills. The salesclerk may simply be supervised by an experienced worker for several days, or there may be an elaborate training program for a "manufacturer's representative." While the training subject matter in retail sales is often not complex, high turnover may still require a high volume of training or supervision, while this high turnover itself may make it appear economically inadvisable to invest too much in any individual worker.[7]

At the other end of the spectrum, a high-technology firm such as Polaroid

Corporation may provide the equivalent of a graduate degree in engineering through some combination of tuition aid and in-house training. Or a General Electric may send an employee to one of its own financial management or engineering schools. In fact, this shadow system of education at these higher-skill and professional levels will often parallel what is offered in higher education, so much so that an accrediting system has been worked out by the American Council of Education and participating companies and colleges/universities whereby employees successfully completing such courses may be awarded academic credit.[8]

Also, among different employers, industries, and even within the same company, there is extreme diversity in how much the schools are looked to as a source of trained employees. Hospitals, for example, employ a great many pharmacists, X-ray technologists, audiologists, and others; untrained non-professionals cannot aspire to those jobs through upgrading.[9] Such untrained workers may qualify for some upgrading training for jobs below the professional level, and increased attention is being given to their training.[10]

In the large Bell Telephone Company system, hiring of workers already trained takes place in only a few occupations, such as clerical, automobile mechanics, and some professional jobs such as lawyers and accountants. These are exceptions to the general practice in which Bell gives initial formal job training and continues training in a highly developed and sophisticated system.[11]

While the Bell system expects to do its own training, a great many other firms expect to hire experienced workers who have acquired their skills in other firms. In a fairly recent Bureau of Labor Statistics study of metalworking industries, more than a quarter of the firms surveyed said they preferred to recruit workers already trained.[12]

The attitudes of employers and unions toward training also vary enormously. The recent survey by Lusterman revealed that the larger employers in the study found training to be a necessary business expense, not primarily a fringe benefit for employees. The report states that "typically, these spokesmen regard all or most of their companies' education and training activities as legitimate and necessary business functions."[13] However, in the same report, a steel company executive is quoted as saying that "training has often been a form of entertainment in industry," and one advocate of training laments that "training is the stepchild of the world of work and is not taken seriously at all."[14]

Organized labor also has varied concerns. Unions are in the forefront of supporting training, and apprenticeship programs are contained in 695 out of 1,570 major collective bargaining agreements analyzed by the Bureau of Labor Statistics in 1976. At the same time, labor unions worry about situations where an excess of trained workers may be created relative to the number of job opportunities, and they fear that where government subsidies exist for training, there may be potential for abuse. A number of union agreements call for advance notification of expected technological changes and the retraining of those workers who would be displaced.[15]

Perhaps the striking diversity in approaches is best evidenced by the wide differences which exist in a single industry. This was the most noteworthy finding in the BLS study of training in metalworking industries:[16]

- In the smallest firms (under 20 employees), under 10 percent provided training, compared to over half in the largest firms (over 1,000 employees).

- Among the large firms, 41.5 percent in electrical machinery provided training, compared to 73 percent in transportation equipment.

- Among the 14 occupations studied, only 1.3 percent of workers in electroplater occupations were enrolled in training, compared to a high of 23.5 percent in welding and frame cutting.

To describe this diversity in training is not to indict it. This review merely illustrates that generalizations about the extent and character of training in American industry are very difficult to make.

Who Trains How Much

Nevertheless, the attempt will be made to piece together a mosaic of training from the snapshots taken from time to time over the last two decades. The problem of measuring the extent of training involves another kind of diversity in industry approaches. The form of training runs from highly informal to highly formal. The bulk of job skills are learned in some manner of on-the-job training. In very informal training, the worker may simply receive some instructions from a supervisor and then be watched over by an experienced worker. But on-the-job training can also be highly structured, with the worker put through a systematic rotation of tasks in order to develop a rounded skill. This on-the-job approach may be combined with classroom training, as in the case of apprenticeship training. Or, many kinds of training may be done chiefly in a classroom setting. Increasingly, workers may be getting job skills outside the firm under tuition-aid programs, explored at length in Chapter 10 of this volume.

The variety of training modes makes measurement very difficult. The more informal varieties are not entered on any records, and the costs are charged to production and not to training budgets. None of the surveys made have really measured this experienced-based means of acquiring skills. But there are successes in measuring the more structured forms of on-the-job training and, of course, the classroom training is susceptible to measurement.

To begin with, there is some indication that more formal methods of training are on the increase. According to one study, exclusive use of informal methods of training declined from 40 percent to 20 percent from 1962 to 1969.[17] What has happened since that time is problematical, although the recent vigorous growth of the American Society for Training and Development suggests that the trend may have continued.

This mosaic of training practices is composed of two kinds of pictures. One comes from the workers themselves, interviewed in household surveys. The other comes from surveys of employers. As for surveys of workers, the primary source of information is unfortunately somewhat dated. The Department of Labor in 1963 surveyed a representative national sample of workers between the ages of 22 and 64.[18] In this survey, the 14 percent of workers who had three or more years of college were treated as a separate population. Of the 86 percent who had less than three years of college, four out of ten said they had received formal training. Of the total worker sample, just over half had received formal training sometime in the course of their lives. Those with less than three years of college were asked what kind of training courses they had completed. Company courses were reported by 6.6 percent, and apprenticeship was the course for 8.2 percent.

When asked what training they had received on their present job, 30 percent reported some formal training and on-the-job training was reported by 56 percent. Forty-five percent learned by casual methods, just by "picking up the job" or from friends and relatives, and 7.5 percent said no training was needed for their jobs. (More than one method was sometimes reported, so the total is greater than 100 percent.) More than half the workers in *all* occupations reported on-the-job learning as the approach they used, except for farm workers, service workers, and laborers, for whom even more casual methods of learning were more common. While the informal methods of training predominate, significant formal training emerges when school, long-term company courses, and short-term and part-time company training are combined.

Workers were also asked which ways of learning they found most helpful for their present job. On-the-job instruction led with 30 percent, only 9 percent said school (which included company courses of six weeks or more, full-time), and 20 percent owed the most to just picking up the job. Eight percent of salesworkers and 3 to 4 percent of most other groups named short company courses or part-time company training. It should be pointed out that both the memories and subjective judgments of workers are involved in such surveys.

The first national survey of employers to explore the character and extent of training in industry was conducted by the Department of Labor in 1962.

Only one out of five establishments reported having formal training (which does not include most on-the-job training), and only 7 percent of the workers were enrolled in such training. The survey's concentration on formal types of classroom training alone unfortunately makes the results less than useful. Half of these enrollees were in some kind of safety training, which, while important, is not job skill training.[19]

While a fairly comprehensive survey of large employers, who are consistently found to offer the most training, took place in 1957, a more comprehensive and recent one was conducted by the Conference Board in 1974–75.[20] Seymour Lusterman included all firms with 500 or more employees, a sample which accounts for about 32 million workers. The survey included *company courses* (whether conducted by the company or outside contract), *tuition-aid programs,* in which the training is selected and arranged for by the employee, and *other outside courses* offered by professional or trade associations and others. Only 22 percent of firms responded to the survey, and among them:[21]

- 89 percent offered tuition aid for after-hours courses;

- 70 percent had company courses during work hours;

- 39 percent had company courses after work hours; and

- 74 percent had other outside courses, during work hours.

As expected, the large firms had the most training, with 96 percent of firms of 10,000 or more employees having company courses during work hours, compared to 55 percent in firms with from 500 to 1,000 employees. While the number of workers participating in training is unclear from the Lusterman report, Harold Goldstein has made estimates, based on the report, that in the firms surveyed the total number of workers involved in formal training was about 6.3 million, or about one out of five of the 32 million workers employed in firms with 500 or more workers.[22]

Participation in company courses varied considerably by industry. Finance ranked highest with 20 percent, manufacturing had a 7 percent participation rate, and the rest were in the 12 percent to 15 percent range. The distribution of expenditures among types of courses was as follows:

Company courses	80%
Outside courses	
Tuition-aid	11%
Other	9%

With respect to who gets the training, Harold Goldstein concludes, based on analysis of the Lusterman data, that training through company courses during working hours (the most prevalent mode) disproportionately emphasizes provision of managerial and other white-collar skills. However, it should again be noted that this survey did not include on-the-job training, the means by which many blue-collar and production employees learn their jobs.

In 1970, the Bureau of Labor Statistics launched a pilot program to test the feasibility of collecting valid statistical data on industrial training. The effort included not only classroom training, but *structured* on-the-job training as well. The survey was only of metalworking industries, electric power, and telephone communications, but firms with as few as 50 employees were included. In this 1970 effort, 41 percent of the metalworking plants reported training, with the differential by size of plant ranging from 32 percent for those with 50 to 249 employees to 71 percent in plants with 1,000 or more employees. This pattern held in the other two industries.[23]

The significance of this BLS survey lies mainly in the fact that collection of data was considered possible. While the survey sampling was quite limited, it evidenced the feasibility of successfully including structured forms of on-the-job training.

The BLS followed this pilot survey with an in-depth survey of fourteen skilled occupations in the metalworking industries, this time including firms with as few as one worker. Unfortunately, however, no tabulation was made by size of plant.[24] Otherwise, the survey provides a wealth of data about skill training in fourteen occupations in the metalworking industries. In 1974, 134,000 workers in these fourteen occupations, or 10 percent of the total employment, enrolled in training. The purpose was predominantly to qualify workers for skilled entry jobs, with 29 percent of training going to skill improvement. The most common mode of training was on the job, with only 31 percent enrolled in training off the production site. Such off-site training was fairly common for welders, however, and nearly half of all training in transportation equipment was off-site.

Putting these bits and pieces together, Harold Goldstein sums it up this way:

> From these diverse surveys, made at different times and including a range of size and classes, a hazy picture emerges: formal training is provided by a good deal less than half of all firms, but by more than 8 out of 10 larger firms (500 employees or more); and the number of workers involved in training in any one year amounts to about one in five in large firms, and a smaller proportion in all industry. Training is mostly given in company-sponsored courses during working hours. Training for skill development (as distinct from orientation, the firm's organization, safety, etc.) is only a part of the total. Much of the formal skill

training is for management or other white collar skills; manual workers get a disproportionately small share of formal training.[25]

It could be added that where the surveys include structured on-the-job training, that mode predominates over classroom training.

As Much As Needed?

Is enough training done to meet industry's needs? If the preceding information about the present investment in training and how that investment has changed over time were complete, we might just begin to answer that question, although such information alone would not speak directly to the adequacy of the investment. But our information is grossly imcomplete. The 1962 survey by the Bureau of Apprenticeship and Training did not touch on-the-job training. The 1977 Conference Board study also excluded on-the-job training and did not include smaller employers. And while the 1974 study by the Bureau of Labor Statistics took a careful approach to measuring such training when it was sufficiently structured to do so, BLS survey work has been limited to skilled occupations in the metalworking industries. Furthermore, none of this accounts for the people who are being trained in terms of who they are and what happens to them afterward.

Therefore, we know almost nothing even about the dollar volume of the private training investment. The Conference Board survey identified a direct cost of $2 billion. The highest estimate of all training, including the wages of workers being trained, is $100 billion in 1975.[26] Harold Goldstein offers an estimate, based on calculations using data from prior studies, of around $10 billion for the cost of private training, but the estimate, he would concede, is no better than the inadequate information on which it is based.[27] Looking at all training, including both public and private and direct and indirect costs (but not wages), the American Society for Training and Development estimates the annual investment at between $30 and $40 billion.[28]

The problem isn't just that the *surveys* have not aggregated training so that it can be summed at the national level or for particular industries or occupations. Corporate and union headquarters do not have the data on which to base future training decisions either, or at least none are in evidence. Even firms committed to training do not have complete records on how much is performed, how much it costs, who gets it, and with what result. This is particularly true because the costs of on-the-job training have not been separated from production costs. For example, Xerox Corporation has made a large commitment to training, but in a case study prepared for the National Institute of Education it was concluded that, as far as how much training Xerox does, "the information needed to answer the question is not collected within Xerox."[29]

How much training should be conducted by industry? Only as much as is needed. It would, on the surface at least, be fair to say that industry obviously trains about as much as it thinks it needs to and about as much as it thinks it can afford, relative to other investments needed to maintain the company's profit position. If the question is whether more data about training are needed simply to supply raw material for academic research, the answer is clear enough: training data are recorded to meet industry production schedules, not as raw material for journal articles. Industry can only be expected to respond to requests for data it does not collect if it can be convinced that such a response would help a legitimate business need. And, since training is a private affair, this conclusion would have to be based on a conviction that there is a possibility of improving efficiency, rather than on any government pronouncements of policy.

Business executives and union leaders would find advantages in having better data about the extent and character of training if the design and collection of data were tailored to meet practical business needs. It seems probable that the current lack of data reflects more a lack of sufficient attention to this area of business operation than any belief that knowing these facts would have no value in making training investment decisions. Nevertheless, it is hard to conclude that training is considered a critical element in the corporate enterprise as long as it is not subjected to any regular accounting and measurement.

There is one feature of the training picture in which the interests of employers, unions, workers, government, and consumers converge. It is regarding the question of what role adequate investments in industrial training play in productivity. The national performance in this area is itself a sufficient basis for examining the state of industrial training as we enter the mid-1980s. It is common knowledge that productivity has seriously declined. From 1948 to 1966, total factor productivity averaged 2.7 percent yearly, falling sharply to 1.3 percent per year for the period 1966–77. In the more familiar "output per person hour" terms, the rate has fallen, over the same time spans, from 3.5 percent per year to 1.9 percent per year.[30]

A declining rate of productivity means an increase in unit costs at a time when inflation is rampant, and it is itself a cause of inflation as these costs are passed on in prices. The decline means slower economic growth and deterioration in the competitive position of the U.S. in foreign markets. Does inadequate training of the American workforce contribute to these productivity trends? Does an increase in training investment for an individual company result in measurable increases in the output per person hour of work? Would companies that do not train reduce their unit costs if they did? For that matter, where companies making like products have different unit costs, are these differences in any way related to how much they train their employees to do their jobs? To our knowledge, none of these questions are answerable now. An executive facing decisions about how much to spend on training has practically nothing solid to go on in making judgments about alternative investments.

With respect to the role of education and training in national economic growth and productivity, the research of productivity experts Edward Denison and John Kendrick raises some intriguing questions about whether greater investments in industrial training could raise productivity. Edward Denison found education to be a significant factor in economic growth from 1929 to 1969.[31] He reached his estimate by first identifying all other factors and then assigning the remaining unexplained residue to education. Using Denison's data but going further, John Kendrick, long experienced in productivity measurement, attempted to measure the effects of education *and* training in more direct ways. Out of a total factor productivity rate of 2.7 percent per year from 1948 to 1966, he ascribes 0.6 percent to education and training. For the period 1966 to 1977, he finds it to account for 0.7 percentage points of the much lower annual rate of 1.3 percent. So in this period of declining productivity, Kendrick's estimates show no slippage due to education and training. There is, of course, no answer here to the question of how responsive productivity would be to *increases* in industrial training. John Kendrick thinks large investments here will help. "In addition to the continued relative growth of private and public outlays for education and training, an increase in the productivity of the resources devoted to these areas is also important."[32]

There should be no advocacy of training based only on some kind of faith that it will perform miracles. Facts are needed to support any hardheaded decisions to become more systematic about training in industry. When we have determined these facts, individual employers and the nation as a whole can decide how much training is needed.

Getting Information

There is sufficient experience to indicate the need for a more systematic approach to getting valid data on the quantity of existing training in individual firms and in the nation. Also, there is enough experience in individual firms with the necessity of training and its role in production to indicate that while attitudes and commitment regarding training vary, a knowledge base for sound decisions would be of value. And there is enough significance in our declining rate of productivity to warrant giving attention to whatever prospect training may have for improving this situation.

Among many individuals and firms, the conviction about training is strong, and harder facts will not make much difference one way or another. But there are other decision-makers who feel the need for more assurance of tangible payoff. The approaches discussed below are designed to provide the underlying base of information and knowledge that will enable more systematic attention to industrial training in the decade of the 1980s.

In-depth Surveys

The approach used in the in-depth survey of the metalworking industry conducted by the Bureau of Labor Statistics after careful pilot testing of measurement techniques could be applied to other industries. The adequate measurement of the quantity and character of industrial training is not easy. It has to be done by people who have intimate knowledge both of the various modes of training and of the structure of industry and industrial processes.

The tentative attempts at measurement of training, begun in the Department of Labor in the early 1960s, slowly evolved into a professional approach that, with continued care and understanding, is now equal to the task of regular and systematic measurement. Industry-by-industry surveys, in depth, would build a base of knowledge about what, in fact, is taking place. The BLS has long been involved in industry studies on a regular basis, although budgetary constraints have seriously limited these efforts. The detailed studies of industry occupation structures made by BLS over the years are a good base on which to build. As industry training studies are repeated from time to time, we will begin to have a sense of what the trends are.

Such studies would require the participation of business and union representatives expert in the industry, especially if the results are to be put to practical use by industry decision-makers.

This is a modest proposal. While there is some attractiveness to the idea of regular national surveys of all industries in a single massive survey, it is unlikely that truly quality data could be obtained in this way. The nature of training varies tremendously among industries, as does the structure of production and the delivery of services. It is likely that more usable information would be produced on an industry-by-industry basis, taking each separately and working with industry advisory committees. Such committees should include not only training officials but also executives with broader responsibilities.

In-depth Case Studies

Statistical surveys alone, however, do not provide the depth of information needed to clarify the role of training in different firms and industries or to provide models for others to examine; a series of careful in-depth case studies of establishments with large training efforts would fill a serious gap. Data on the absolute quantity of different types of training need to be supplemented by looking at training in the total context of the enterprise—how it fits into the system of production, how it ties to personnel and staffing systems, and how it is related to changes in production methods and technology. There also needs to be a better tracing through of the benefits that stem from quality training programs in terms of output, unit labor costs, etc.

These case studies should be undertaken only by people who have knowledge of the structure of industry and industrial processes, and they would need to involve a broad spectrum of firm executives, supervisors, and workers. There would have to be free access to necessary records. Such case studies would best be undertaken by individuals and organizations outside of the government, although government support for the effort would be appropriate, particularly if supplemented by private financial support.

Study of Training and Productivity

If there were careful, systematic investigations of the role training plays in industry productivity, we could get beyond the "folk knowledge" phase we are now in. A lot of people have an opinion about the role training plays in productivity, but this author has yet to see a convincing fact. While there is certainly a common-sense basis for the proposition that learning the right way to do a job will get it done better, a great many decision-makers want something solid, because there are dollar outlays involved, as well as the diversion of personnel from production to training status. And common sense is not *always* reliable. The admonition to look before you leap is matched by the advice that he who hesitates is lost.

While economists would be interested in the effect training has on the traditional productivity measure of "output per person hour," this is not a measure that would necessarily have meaning to individual employers. The studies of results should be related to the kinds of indicators of well-being employers use to measure results.

A Training and Productivity Center

There is a need for a Training and Productivity Center, based in the private sector, to be a vehicle for stimulating the kind of efforts recommended above, to assure that private sector involvement is arranged, and to serve as a source for information about training results and successful practices. There needs to be a place where research combines with action and where an objective view of the returns to training investments can be obtained. Such a center would not assume an advocacy role for training but rather would provide whatever facts can be ascertained. Its expertise would be in (1) successful training models, (2) measures of the extent of training in industry of various types, and

(3) knowledge of how levels of training investment affect the bottom line of the corporate financial statement.

Employer Feedback

To the extent that employers find the products of schools not sufficiently prepared in the basics, they need to become involved at the local level to press for adequate educational resources and the best application of them. Many employers believe they have a legitimate concern about the extent to which the schools' products have deficiencies in basic education or in skill training, for graduates of vocational and occupational training. But employment institutions and educational institutions have grown apart, and the communication system is inadequate to mobilize the resources of the employing community to address this problem.

The adequacy of youth development is not the sole responsibility of the public schools. All community institutions have a responsibility for, and a stake in, a successful transition from school to work. The best way to work on the problem is for employers to take the lead in urging joint education, labor, and industry collaboration at the local level in supportive actions. Such efforts are underway in some communities in the form of Industry-Education-Labor Councils or Community Education Work Councils. They offer models for the employing community wherever present practices do not produce adequate results.

* * * *

No one can say exactly what the state of training is within industry in 1980, how that compares with 1970 or 1930, and what, if anything, should be done differently in the future. Industry training is too diverse for generalizations, and each firm's approach to training is a private concern.

But what is left after this distillation of bits and pieces of knowledge is the uncomfortable feeling that, in general, employers operate more with "folk knowledge" about the role of training in industrial production and productivity than with the hard evidence we assume the business manager demands. The time has come to work seriously at compiling more complete information on how different approaches and levels of training affect productivity, unit labor costs, job satisfaction, and the like. We enter the mid-1980s in the midst of a decline in productivity at a time when we can ill afford it. And there is a future ahead in which high energy-consuming approaches to production, which have raised productivity by simply lowering the labor input, will not be as available as in the past. Can we afford not to develop the human resource as much as possible, when our natural resources are in increasingly short supply?

In spite of what might seem to be a common-sense conclusion that we should press hard on the training front as a countermeasure to adverse energy and productivity trends, we have stopped short of the exhortation to "Train! Train! Train!" Those who now believe that training will in fact raise productivity are either beginning or enlarging training. Those who do not now make substantial investments will not respond to mere exhortation, but will want to know what they can expect to get for their investments. So we have suggested a knowledge-building approach, coupled with practical ways to get good information into the hands of those who can use it.

Considerable note has been taken of the interplay between the education and training provided by the public authorities and that provided by industry. How well the job of educating is done before prospective workers show up in the hiring office has a lot to do with how much and what kind of education and training industry has to offer. Employers more frequently are voicing complaints about the basic education of the young people coming to them. We have suggested that employers need to take initiatives to get these problems resolved through a collaborative approach with education and labor organizations at the local level. There are many models to build on here in Industry-Education-Labor Councils and Community Education Work Councils.

The Industrial Revolution and advanced technology have broken jobs into sufficiently small components so as to both simplify the worker's task and reduce the need for human labor. This approach to productivity may have made us much less attentive to how we can raise the performance of workers through investments in human resources. The future will not afford us the luxury of pushing forward only on the basis of what energy-using machines can do without careful attention to what workers can do with brains and hands.

Notes

1   Ernest Bogart and Donald Kemmerer, *Economic History of the American People,* Longmans, Green and Co., 1942, p. 83.
2   Quoted in Daniel Bell, *Work and Its Discontents,* New York: League for Industrial Democracy, 1970.
3   U.S. Bureau of the Census, Series P–20, No. 274, Table 1.
4   For a full description of the operation of this "internal labor market" see Peter Doeringer and Michael Piore, *Internal Labor Markets and Manpower Analyses,* Lexington, Mass.: D.C. Heath and Co., 1971.
5   Peter Doeringer and Michael Piore, *Internal Labor Markets, Technological Change, and Labor Force Adjustment,* Report submitted to Office of Manpower Policy, Evaluation and Research, U.S. Department of Labor, Cambridge, Mass., 1966.
6   Seymour Lusterman, *Education in Industry,* New York: The Conference Board, 1977, p. 6.
7   Harold Clark and Joe Davis, "Training in Business and Industry," in *Developing The Nation's Work Force,* Yearbook 5, ed. Merle E. String, American Vocational Association, Washington, D.C., 1975.

8 See *The National Guide to Credit Recommendations for Non-Collegiate Courses,* 1978 edition, American Council on Education.
9 U.S. Department of Labor, *Occupational Outlook Handbook,* 1978–79 edition, pp. 447–515.
10 D. L. Kimmerly, Vice-President, Human Resources, Michael Reese Hospital and Medical Center, Chicago, at a National Institute of Education Conference on Workplace Education and Training, 1979.
11 W. Frank Blount, in testimony before the U.S. Senate Committee on Labor and Human Resources, June 6–7, 1979.
12 U.S. Department of Labor, Bureau of Labor Statistics and Employment and Training Administration, *Occupational Training in Selected Metal-Working Industries,* BLS Bulletin 1976, FTA R&D Monograph 53, 1977, pp. 11–13.
13 Lusterman, p. 1.
14 Thomas Gilbert, "Training: The $100 Billion Opportunity," *Training and Development Journal,* Nov. 1976, p. 4.
15 Harvey Belitsky, *Productivity and Job Security: Retraining to Adapt to Technological Change,* National Center for Productivity and Quality of Working Life, Washington, D.C.: The Center, 1977, p. 9.
16 *Occupational Training.*
17 Bureau of National Affairs survey, cited by Clark and Davis.
18 *Formal Occupational Training of Adult Workers,* U.S. Department of Labor, Office of Manpower, Automation, and Training, 1964.
19 *Training of Workers in American Industry,* 1962, U.S. Department of Labor, Bureau of Apprenticeship and Training, Washington, D.C., 1965.
20 For the results of the 1957 study, see Harold Clark and Harold Sloan, *Classrooms in the Factories: An Account of Educational Activities Conducted by American Industry,* Rutherford, N.J.: Fairleigh Dickinson University, 1958.
21 Lusterman, Table 2.6. For a discussion of treatment of nonresponse and adjustments not included by Mr. Lusterman, see Harold Goldstein, *Training and Education by Industry,* National Manpower Institute, 1979, p. 28.
22 For a full explanation of the estimate, see Goldstein, pp. 28–29.
23 James Neary, "The BLS Pilot Survey of Training in Industry," *Monthly Labor Review,* February 1974, pp. 26–32.
24 *Occupational Training.*
25 Goldstein, p. 34.
26 Gilbert, pp. 3–8.
27 Goldstein, pp. 38–39.
28 *National Report for Training and Development,* American Society for Training and Development, Vol. 5, No. 11, 1979.
29 John Dinkelspiel, "Industry Training Strategies: A Case Study of Xerox Corporation," paper presented at the NIE Workshop on Education and Training Policy, Washington, D.C., 1979, p. 6.
30 John Kendrick, "Increasing Productivity," in *Inflation and National Survival,* ed. Clarence Walton, New York: The Academy of Political Science, 1979, p. 191.
31 Edward Denison, *Accounting for United States Economic Growth, 1929–1969,* The Brookings Institution, 1974.
32 Kendrick, p. 196.

Chapter 7

Labor Unions, Education, and Training

We need Educare for the mind as we need Medicare for the body.

> Albert Shanker, President, American Federation of Teachers, 1979

Today, it appears that particularly in America, the Colleges go in for vocational and professional education to the utter neglect of a genuine liberal education. Workers' education in its integrative aspect is endeavoring to see the whole life of man, to preserve the total personality. . . . Workers' education is a challenge to all workers by hand and brain to become the masters of social direction.

> Marius Hansome, *World Workers' Educational Movements,* 1931

Education is an investment in the future of America: an investment in people that pays rich dividends through a better trained, more productive work force, and an informed citizenry. . . . The goal of the AFL-CIO is equal access to all levels of education for every American who seeks and can benefit from that education.

> Walter Davis, Director of Education, AFL-CIO, 1977

Today we must extend . . . education so we can make science and technology and our vast industrial structures help us move into a democratic society where all the people, fully informed, with complete access to the entire culture, have equal opportunity to share in the future, its material benefits, its spiritual rewards, and its cultural richness.

> Carroll Hutton, Director of Education, United Auto Workers, 1977

The goals of organized workers are not easily distinguished from those of other organizations and citizens that support the ideas of a well-educated democratic citizenry and equality of opportunity through access to education. For organized labor, views about education are in the mainstream of American values and aspirations. Historically, organized labor led in the battle to spread educational opportunity to all citizens.

Because unions are involved in education on so many fronts, and since educational opportunity is so central to union objectives, it is not easy to describe the labor movement's role in education in one chapter. Union interest in education extends to all the aspects of worklife learning covered elsewhere in this volume. This chapter has the limited objective of describing the union role overall, for its scope is not as widely appreciated as it needs to be by those interested in expanding learning opportunity during working life. We are not concerned here with the important matter of workers' receiving adequate instruction in the administration or negotiation of collective bargaining contracts. Rather, this chapter attempts to paint the larger picture of union activity and objectives, including the union as an advocate of public education, as an educational institution, as a negotiator for education benefits, and as a collaborator with, and critic of, higher education.

A History of Advocacy

Efforts of organized labor to expand education proceeded on two fronts, the development of workers' education and the advocacy of general public education. Workers' education or labor education (in the United States the two terms are used interchangeably) is a specialized branch of adult education that attempts to meet educational needs and interests arising out of workers' participation in the union movement.[1]

Twenty-five years ago Joseph Mire described workers' education as

> an education carried on either under direct union auspices or education carried on by nonlabor agencies jointly with union groups. Its objectives are the improvement of the worker's individual and group competence and the advancement of his social, economic, and cultural interests so that he can become a mature, wise, and responsible citizen able to play his part in the union and in a free society and to assure for himself a status of dignity and respect equal to those of other groups and individuals.[2]

Workers' education programs took root in the United States as early as 1903. Despite the fact that the decade of the 1920s represented a period of decline in union membership, the number of institutions providing labor education grew. This period was marked by the creation of education departments in the International Ladies Garment Workers Union (1917) and the Amalgamated Clothing Workers Association (1919), and by the founding of the Workers' Education Bureau of America in New York City (1921). During the decade, about 300 labor colleges existed whose sponsorship ranged across the ideological spectrum from radical political parties to conservative state universities.[3] Although labor colleges were often discontinued as the unions lost strength, some persevered, and there was an increase in the number of independent labor agencies, particularly resident schools such as Bryn Mawr, Brookwood, and the Rand School.

What is most fascinating about this educational movement today is the degree to which it represented a genuine grass-roots quest for knowledge of how the society and economy operated and how little it was connected with occupational and economic advancement in the labor market. There is in this early experience a basis for understanding why labor unions today urge that education be widely available to workers and not be limited to skills training and upgrading. The strength of this feeling in the early movement is illustrated by the policy of the Workers' Bookshelf of the Workers' Education Bureau (WEB), which stated in 1925 that it would

> contain no volumes on trade training nor books which gave shortcuts to material success. The reasons which will finally determine the selection of titles for the Workers' Bookshelf will be because they enrich life, because they illumine the human experience, and because they deepen human understanding.[4]

Such a policy sounds almost foreign in contemporary adult education circles where so much attention is focused upon occupational advancement of one kind or another. Much of today's popular reading, such as *What Color Is Your Parachute?* and *Watching Out for Number One,* would have been banned by the above criteria from the WEB bookshelves. There would have been no support in that era for the current trend toward making more and more of postsecondary education specific to occupational and professional job skills.

Workers' education in the United States underwent a major expansion in the 1930s, although the content changed. The enormous influx of new members into trade unions in the late 1930s resulted in a need to teach the new recruits how to organize, lead, and administer effective trade unions. This was particularly true of the newly organized mass production unions. The labor movement responded to this need by developing educational programs dealing with the nuts-and-bolts issues of trade union organization and day-to-day union work. During this period, the major agencies of worker education became the trade unions themselves, while the role of independent educational agencies declined because much of their funding was drying up during the Depression.[5]

The other major goal of organized labor throughout the twentieth century was to promote public education and to extend its reach. According to Melvin Barlow, a historian of industrial and vocational education, one of the three major forces that produced federally-supported vocational education in 1917 (the Smith-Hughes Act) was the work of the Committee on Education of the American Federation of Labor.[6] This tradition was continued as the late Peter Schoemann, Chairman of the ALF-CIO Standing Committee on Education, played a major role in shaping and securing the 1963 amendments to the Vocational Education Act, a major revision of vocational education policy.[7]

In supporting public education and its improvement, the AFL-CIO has continued to insist that education be as broadly defined as possible, and that occupational education in its narrowest sense be opposed, particularly if it closes off opportunities at an early age. While the AFL-CIO supported the enactment of the Career Education Incentive Act in 1977, it raised some cautionary notes at the same time:

> The focus of career education should be on widening the career options which are available to students rather than trying to freeze the student into a single trade or occupation. . . . The goal of education should be to teach the flexibility that can help the individual adjust to change.[8]

During recent years, organized labor has supported both the Elementary and Secondary Education Act and the Higher Education Act.

The educational goals of organized labor have shown considerable consistency throughout this century. Those goals have been within the mainstream of American concern for an educated citizenry, and future union efforts to advance worklife learning can be expected to continue this long tradition.

Unions as Learning Institutions

The emphasis of trade union educational activity has shifted at times, depending on the exigencies of the situations in which trade unions have found themselves. As noted above, the general social purpose of workers' education gave way in the 1930s when unions faced with the influx of millions of new members focused on teaching the fundamentals of trade union organization and leadership to these new recruits. Starting in the late 1940s, with the consolidation of the labor movement organizationally, broader issues in workers' education once again assumed a prominent place in trade union educational activities, especially in their cooperative relationships with universities and other institutions of higher learning.

While much labor union education remains concerned with passing on the tools of the trade in union affairs, educational efforts have grown to include much more, encompassing even the liberal arts. Even occupationally-related labor education may lead workers to seek more education, because it gets them started on some practical, easily recognized need. This point is emphasized by John MacKenzie of the Center for Educational Services:

> Although these courses that assist them at the workplace or within their union are the initial attraction, many workers move on to obtain further education, often with the counseling assistance of a labor educator. The point is that the labor education courses serve as a catalyst to spur many workers to further their education. Labor education was not designed to provide an educational intake system for workers, but it is now one of its current functions.[9]

Unions now spend millions from union dues to provide educational services in a wide variety of settings. An estimated 20,000 workers attend one-week residential institutes, and approximately 50,000 shop stewards, committeepeople, and local union officers attend weekend seminars. These seminars are conducted by the AFL-CIO Education Department or the education departments of international unions.[10] Herbert Levine describes these institutes and seminars as providers of "increased knowledge and understanding of economic, social, and political issues," as well as of instruction concerning the role of a union member.[11]

In a 1967 study of more than 180 national unions, 40 unions representing more than 18 million workers reported sponsoring some educational activities. That year, 34 of the 40 unions reported the employment of 192 persons to work on education programs, 94 of them full-time. Forty-two of the 192 employees worked for a single union.[12] This study is somewhat dated; it would be useful to have more recent data on the scope of labor union efforts. But the point that union educational commitment and activity is extensive is still valid today.

One of the most expansive views of the role of labor unions in education is set forth in a presentation by Carroll Hutton, Director of the Education Department of the United Auto Workers, entitled "In the Era of Lifetime Learning, the UAW Is a Learning Community." According to Mr. Hutton, we can no longer "limit our knowledge to the plant management; we have to know more about economics, more about the nature of international trade, more about the effects of noise and dirt and pressure and stress on our ability to survive."[13]

The most comprehensive educational effort of the UAW is the operation of the Family Educational Center at Black Lake, Michigan. As the name implies, education is for the whole family; the approach is just one example of a pervasive union attitude favoring educational services for spouses and children. The range of educational activities offered by the UAW includes a language program at a number of UAW locals for immigrant workers who cannot speak English. Local 600 Vice-President Ernie Lofton got his local involved in this program when one worker was almost injured. "When someone yelled 'Look Out' for a hazard, he didn't understand the words and narrowly escaped being hurt."[14]

Two major educational activities are carried on by the AFL-CIO. It operates the George Meany Labor Studies Center in Silver Spring, Maryland, offering a very wide range of courses from art appreciation to labor law, though concentrating heavily on tool courses. Through a cooperative arrangement with Antioch College, credit is available for these courses. The AFL-CIO also makes resource materials available to its member unions, prepares materials for labor education programs, maintains a film library, and conducts colleges and special programs.[15]

A recent union educational venture is the Pacific Northwest Labor College, in a suburb of Portland, Oregon, started in 1977 by AFL-CIO unions, unaffiliated labor organizations, and employee associations. Its basic mission is to provide lifelong learning programs for workers of all ages and to carry on whatever educational efforts are needed to advance and enhance the lives of workers.[16] A liberal arts college, a branch campus of the College of New Rochelle in New York, has been established by District Council 37 of the American Federation of State, County, and Municipal Employees. Another union-sponsored college is that of District 65 of the Distributive Workers Union, in collaboration with Hofstra University, also in New York State. Yet another in New York is the Labor College, supported by the Central Labor Council.[17]

While the largest growth in "labor studies centers" at the postsecondary level has occurred in universities and community colleges (about which more is said later), labor unions are themselves directly offering a wide range of educational services. Today, no index of higher education offerings would be complete without a growing list of union courses.

In addition to providing education directly, some unions have been pioneers in providing support services to link workers with learning opportunities. A ground-breaking effort to channel more educational opportunities to rank-and-file workers and help provide the counseling they need to take advantage of these opportunities was the Educational Advancement Program run by the International Union of Electricians (IUE) from 1969 to 1972, with funding from the Department of Labor. At the time, the program represented a wholly new approach; it preceded attempts in the late 1970s to deliver counseling and educational opportunity to workers more effectively. The objectives were to identify the education and training needs of IUE-represented workers, demonstrate that workers can be recruited for education, provide career guidance, determine impact of education, and reach minority workers.

The results were considerable. With more than 8,000 workers involved, basic education was provided to 146, General Education Diplomas to 860, clerical and vocational training to 3,600, "union-related" instruction to 2,175, college-level work to 230, and miscellaneous other subjects to 900. The per pupil costs were held to between $35 and $46.[18] The experience of the IUE would be valuable for any union today desiring to launch a comprehensive educational program for its members. The program required the collaboration of the union, the employer, and the educational institutions in the community.

As extensive as direct educational programs operated unilaterally by unions are becoming, the more pervasive impact on educational opportunity for workers will probably be through the benefits negotiated in collective bargaining contracts.

Union as Negotiator for Education and Training

Three-quarters of a century ago, in describing the primary goals of the American Federation of Labor, Samuel Gompers simply said "more." Today, that includes more education and training, as well as more pay and better working conditions. Not that bargaining for education and training has the same importance as traditional bread-and-butter issues, but their presence on the agenda may be a growing phenomenon in the 1980s.

There is, of course, a considerable history of collective bargaining for education and training benefits. It has produced the formal apprenticeship system, a tried-and-true method of training for centuries. Apprenticeship programs are jointly sponsored by employers and unions (although many smaller ones are offered unilaterally by employers), and provide a combination of planned, supervised on-the-job training and related classroom instruction. The duration of the apprenticeship varies from one to six years, depending on the craft or skill involved.

Apprenticeship training is now available in about 415 recognized skill occupations. This skill training takes place in approximately 41,000 registered programs and involves about 400,000 apprentices, although 82 percent of these programs are sponsored by employers without union participation. However, because joint union-employer programs are usually larger, they train the majority of apprentices.[19] The federal government encourages apprenticeship programs under the National Apprenticeship Act of 1937, which established a federal Bureau of Apprenticeship and Training to promote labor standards that protect apprentices, bring together employers and unions to encourage sponsorship of programs, and cooperate with state agencies having similar missions.

Efforts have been underway for some time to increase the participation of minorities and women in apprenticeship programs. While minorities now constitute around 17 percent of enrollments, women still account for only about 2 percent, although even this is a considerable increase.[20] This effort has been greatly facilitated through the Apprenticeship Outreach Program worked out by the AFL-CIO Building Trades Department in 1968, "under which churches, civil rights groups, schools, and other organizations recruited minority youth and helped them to meet the requirements of apprenticeship."[21]

Although apprenticeship is generally thought of as primarily intended for youth, it is included in this discussion of adult worklife learning. In fact, the average apprentice is 25 years old, has been out of high school for about seven years, and is in other ways more like a working adult than a youth still in the school system.

Much less attention has been paid to upgrading the skills of journeymen than to initial apprenticeship, although substantial upgrading programs exist. An example is the upgrading training for journeymen members of the International Union of Operating Engineers. In this program, one or two expert journeymen serve as instructors in the operation of a piece of new equipment at the worksite. Such efforts may be much more formal, such as a week-long course explaining the use of a single piece of equipment. The training may also feature the dealer providing equipment and instruction on its use in special "company" courses.

A study of workers being upgraded in 41 local construction unions in eight cities found the participants in such skill upgrading programs enthusiastic, but also made a number of recommendations for improvement. The first recommendation was for the union to take greater pains to inform the members of upgrading opportunities, since one out of six members interviewed had been unaware of the opportunities. Union members also cited problems with commuting to classes after work as a reason for not attending.[22]

A more recent joint effort between unions and employers is the negotiated tuition-aid plan. It allows workers to go to school and either receive a tuition reimbursement after completing their courses, or, under a few plans, receive a payment for tuition before beginning courses (tuition aid is discussed in detail in Chapter 10). In its 1978 study, *An Untapped Resource,* the National Manpower Institute (NMI, now the National Institute for Work and Learning) identified 198 such negotiated tuition-aid plans, covering approximately 1.6 million workers.[23] These plans are found in all types of industries: 54 percent in manufacturing, 18 percent in transportation and utilities, 19 percent in service industries, and 9 percent in construction.

While most plans provide that the employer reimburse workers for tuition costs, the NMI study identified 21 "training fund plans" in which employers contribute fixed amounts of money per worker to a central fund that finances education and training opportunities. These funds are usually administered by a board of trustees as part of an industry-wide or area-wide program.[24] An example of a very successful training fund program administered by a union (through a board of trustees composed of union members) is that of District Council 37 of the American Federation of State, County, and Municipal Employees. Contributions to the Education Fund are made by the New York City government and amount to $25 per eligible worker. Education Fund programs serve about 3,000 students per week, and many of the courses are oversubscribed.[25]

While paid educational leave and leave of absence plans are not extensive in this country, there are a few that have been negotiated between unions and employers. The NMI study identified 13 negotiated plans containing such provisions. These plans operate in conjunction with tuition reimbursement. Educational leave is granted for a specified period during working hours and is therefore paid for. Leave of absence is usually granted for an extended period of time with or without full or partial wage maintenance.

Paid educational leave is much more frequently negotiated in Europe than in the United States.[26] From the union and worker standpoint, it does have the merit of providing time for workers to go back to school, which removes a barrier to participation in education. From the employer's standpoint, it is a costly arrangement and can also make work scheduling more difficult. There are also clear benefits in terms of upgrading workforce skills. High technology corporations have sometimes found the benefits to outweigh the costs. The United Auto Workers in Canada recently negotiated a paid educational leave agreement that could have a ripple effect below the border.[27]

Another model of a joint union and employer education and training effort is the Harry Lundeberg School of Seamanship, founded at Piney Point, Maryland, in 1967. The Lundeberg School trains inland boatmen and seafarers and is the largest of its kind in the U.S. All funds for the school are secured through collective bargaining. Thirty deep-sea companies and 100 towing companies contribute to the school through contractual agreements with the Seafarers International Union. There are no educational requirements for entry, and activity has grown to the point where 1,082 men and women were graduated in 1978.[28]

The need for such an effort was put succinctly by the school's president, Hazel P. Brown:

> The maritime industry will continue to face the increased use of automation and advanced technology. With these technological advances, the maritime workers are faced with acquiring more sophisticated skills and life adjustment techniques. As more workers will need a higher level of educational experiences, a greater burden will be placed upon union and management for additional funds to be negotiated through the collective bargaining process for use in training and educational benefits rather than providing additional take-home wages.[29]

The collective bargaining arrangements which support the Lundeberg school offer an unusual example of the centralization of training across an industry, financed through the mechanism of collective bargaining.

The array of education and training opportunities secured through the collective bargaining process has grown to include traditional apprenticeship programs; programs to upgrade the skills of journeymen; negotiated tuition-aid plans; educational training fund plans administered by unions, but contributed to by employers; paid educational leave and leave of absence arrangements for educational purposes; and whole educational and training institutions serving the skill needs of a large number of individual employers within an industry.

Unions and Higher Education

Unions are both strong critics of higher education, and increasingly, its collaborators. In either situation, the goals are the same: to extend educational opportunity to workers and to develop and increase the effectiveness of union leaders. This growing collaboration is viewed with ambivalence by many union officials. Strong reservations are expressed by Gus Tyler of the International Ladies Garment Workers, a long-time leader of the labor movement in the area of education: "I have some genuine anxieties about the marriage between unions and academies, and they center on three perils: the commercialization of credits, the corruptions of communication, and the misuse of ideology."[30]

Mr. Tyler's first concern is quality; as higher education expands to more nontraditional students, "the whole process may just become a diploma mill." His second concern is communication, that "too many faculty members will turn off workers-students because the professor can only talk, and think, in the arcane argot of the academic tribe." Third, he is concerned about the "ideological emptiness" of the social sciences as they are usually taught.[31]

Another criticism of higher education is that it simply has not taken the trouble to be responsive to worker needs:

> Trade unionists point out that professional educators have spent billions of federal dollars over the past decades in research, experimentation, and demonstration programs which have received the legislative support of trade unions. Yet these same professional educators have not researched the educational needs of some 20 million Americans who belong to trade unions, nor do they seem aware that there are 180,000 local union officers and thousands of staff and professional persons at work in the labor movement. Professional educators, even at this late date, are not accustomed to working with union leaders.[32]

Despite a variety of reservations about higher education, collaborative relations are expanding, sometimes with unions more eager than education institutions for such joint efforts. This was the situation seen by the UAW in 1975 when Leonard Woodcock observed that "the fact that the UAW has undertaken cooperative programs with only about 30 community colleges indicates not that the UAW has been shy, but rather that most of the community colleges have held back in entering into ambitious ventures with the UAW and other unions."[33] However true this statement in 1975, more recent trends show considerable enthusiasm on the part of community colleges.

But the story of collaboration begins with the four-year institutions rather than with the two-year ones. As indicated above, unions and universities collaborated in developing workers' education programs as early as the 1920s, but this cooperation reached a new, higher level in the 1940s and one which has been expanding ever since. Between 1956 and 1967, universities developed long-term, noncredit liberal arts programs for labor. Rutgers University, Penn State, and West Virginia University cooperated in the development of a four-year union leadership academy. Cornell University developed a liberal-arts-for-labor program and the United Steelworkers Union and Indiana University developed a six-month residential credit program. The Communication Workers of America also experimented during this period with a ten-week staff training institute. Each of these programs in their own way represented innovations in such collaborative ventures.

Furthermore, several universities began seriously to develop degree-granting programs by the mid 1960s. For example, Rutgers University, Penn State, and the University of Massachusetts were among the pioneers in this area.

The goals of the new degree programs in universities are broad, and although varied, are described by a leader in university programs as "aimed at helping the worker to become (1) a better individual; (2) a contributing member of his (her) own union group; and (3) a participating citizen in the community."[34] A significant distinction of labor studies programs is that they offer college credit and grant degrees. The program at the University of Massachusetts was the first, granting a master's degree in labor studies in 1965. Rutgers University offered a B.A. in labor studies through its evening college in 1967 and subsequently developed an M.A. and M.Ed. and an Ed.D. program in Labor Education. Today, about 47 colleges and universities offer a major or concentration in labor studies.[35] This trend toward college credit is not embraced by all labor educators, and some national union education directors have also expressed reservations.

One unique program is the Weekend College at Wayne State University in Michigan. It enrolls about 3,000 workers in liberal studies programs for credit, and provides instructional approaches that include television and discussion meetings in union halls.[36] "Dual enrollment" programs between unions and community colleges represent another innovative and promising approach.

The International Union of Operating Engineers, through its National Joint Apprenticeship and Training Committee, is the leader in dual enrollment efforts. It provides college study simultaneously with apprenticeship. Program participants meet the requirements both for the regular apprenticeship program and for an associate degree at a community college.

The Operating Engineers, in cooperation with participating community colleges, started the dual enrollment program in 1972 with a grant from the Department of Labor. The program proposal stated that "the essence of education is to permit an individual to become all that he (she) may become, limited only by talent and ambition. The construction industry and our country need individuals with a broad base of knowledge of the industry and their trade, as well as a general preparation for a role as an enlightened member of society." The individual programs are worked out by the local Joint Apprenticeship Training Council and a community college. The union selects the college after a survey "to determine which [college] could best meet the criteria of breadth and flexibility of course offerings, receptivity to the philosophy of the program, and comparatively modest cost to the student."[37]

Beyond these specialized programs, community college involvement with labor studies has undergone a lot of growth in recent years. The degree of interest is evidenced by the fact that the American Association of Community and Junior Colleges (AACJC) has created a Service Center for Community–Labor Union Cooperation.

In 1977, the AACJC asked community colleges about their involvement with unions and labor studies education. Forty-one percent of the responding institutions said they had developed programs at the request of employers. Sixty-five percent said they had union members on their advisory committees, and 21 percent had union leaders as trustees. In more than a quarter of the programs, the colleges sponsor off-campus activities at either the place of work, union halls, community centers, or high schools.[38] Almost four out of ten colleges are involved in apprenticeship training programs. The potential role of community colleges in the education of workers and union members was identified by Leonard Woodcock, President of the United Auto Workers, in an address to the AACJC convention in 1975: "We regard the American community college as the late twentieth century counterpart of the free public schools that workers and their unions struggled to create and expand in the 19th century."

Unions and higher education institutions are more frequently identifying their common interests and working out their differences. It is a development that most surely should be encouraged to extend opportunities for learning during working life.

Policies for the 1980s

The prospects for providing workers with increased options for learning throughout working life are substantially brightened as labor unions press forward on educational agendas drawn up in the 1960s and 1970s. There are a number of problems and barriers to enlarging these opportunities to whose resolution unions can contribute substantially.

- There is the need to get information to the worker about opportunities that exist in his or her community. Unions are in the ideal position to be conduits of information to about 20 million workers. The union may initiate information gathering, but those institutions that offer education and training to adults and workers would be well advised to initiate their own contacts with unions and enlist them in disseminating information.

- There is the need for workers to have ready access to someone who knows what the opportunities are and how to negotiate for them. One promising approach is to train "learning organizers," union members and officers who will be available to assist workers. They can operate at workplaces in collaboration with management and in union halls.

- There is the need for academic institutions to be sensitive to the learning requirements of workers who have had little involvement with educational institutions since they left high school, and whose experience even then may have been less than rewarding. Many of these workers may well have learning styles that are different and may feel much more comfortable in workplace, community, or union settings. The union can press educational institutions to reach out to workers and learn from them their wants and needs.

- There is the need to maintain quality as postsecondary educational institutions press forward to enroll the "nontraditional" student. While the actual "selling" of degrees may be easy to recognize, more subtle attempts to give very little education and some form of academic certification in exchange for money are not as easily identified. If unions were to take a close interest in what these educational institutions are doing, it would be a constructive development.

In collective bargaining, unions can be expected to bargain for what they perceive workers to want. There is a growing perception that workers in many places want some of their benefits package in the form of increased opportunity for education and training. The fact that there are increasingly more bargains on education benefits being struck between unions and employers suggests that there is mutual interest in these benefits. In the United States, there has been only limited public support for the education and training of adults. After public school, the decision has been left to American industry—the employer and the labor union—and to the individual as to whether he or she pays tuition at a school, college, or private training institute. Whether or not the United States sees a significant expansion in worklife learning may well depend on the relative rank of education and training benefits in the total pay and benefits package.

Where public support for worklife learning exists, we should be looking toward a pluralistic approach to the identification of needs and the delivery of education and training services. Labor unions have established themselves over the decades as responsible deliverers of educational services. The history of labor's involvement with education shows that it is well within the mainstream of American judgment and opinion about the importance and role of education in an industrial democracy. Laws which provide governmental support should recognize that labor unions, as well as other institutions, have a legitimate role in worklife learning. One model for legislative action is the federal Lifelong Learning Act of 1976 which, for all practical purposes, has never been financed.

* * * *

Organized labor has been in pursuit of organized learning throughout its history. The form that pursuit has taken has varied from time to time. But it has never swerved from strong advocacy of a system of universal education accessible to all, based on the provision of equal opportunity and free from the early tracking and closing of opportunities traditional in industrial countries such as the United Kingdom and West Germany. Organized labor has been a direct provider of education and training, has negotiated with management to make education a part of the benefits package, and has cooperated with some 95 institutions of higher education. Labor has strongly criticized American higher education's "half-hearted response" to the needs of the working force, even as it has increasingly collaborated with higher education to expand opportunities for workers.

Labor unions have been a strong force in shaping a learning society, and have the potential for remaining so, depending on how high a value they place on education and training in the total economic picture.

Notes

[1]   Larry Rogin and Marjorie Rachlin, *Labor Education in the United States,* National Institute of Labor Education, September, 1968, p. 11.

2 Joseph Mire, *Labor Education,* Inter-university Labor Education Committee, Strauss Printing Company, 1956.

3 Richard Dwyer, "Workers' Education, Labor Education, Labor Studies: An Historical Delineation," *Review of Educational Research,* Winter, 1977, p. 183.

4 *National University Extension Association Proceedings,* 1925, p. 45.

5 Rogin and Rachlin, pp. 19–20.

6 Melvin Barlow, *The Unconquerable Senator Page,* American Vocational Association, 1976.

7 Walter Davis, Director, Department of Education, AFL-CIO, in testimony before the U.S. House of Representatives Subcommittee on Elementary, Secondary, and Vocational Education, March 2, 1977.

8 Walter Davis.

9 John R. MacKenzie, "The Supply of Learning Opportunities for Workers," Center for Educational Services, a paper prepared for the Department of Health, Education and Welfare's Lifelong Learning Project, 1977.

10 Herbert Levine and Morris Fried, "Expanding Options for Worker Education," in *Implementing New Education Work Policies,* ed. Paul E. Barton, San Francisco: Jossey-Bass, 1978, p. 74.

11 Levine and Fried, p. 75.

12 Lawrence Rogin and Marjorie Rachlin, *Survey of Adult Education Opportunities for Labor,* National Institute of Labor Education and The American University, Final Report to the U.S. Office of Education, September, 1968, p. 4.

13 Carroll M. Hutton, Director, Education Department, International Union, United Auto Workers, in a presentation to UAW Region 1E, Labor Education Graduating Class, Taylor, Michigan, June 26, 1977, p. 4.

14 "Union Teaches Them a New Language," *Solidarity,* 22, No. 2, March 5, 1979.

15 "Citizen Education in a Union Setting," University and College Labor Education Association, prepared for the U.S. Office of Education, February 1978, p. 9.

16 *AFL-CIO News,* February 3, 1979.

17 Lois S. Gray, "Academic Degrees for Labor Studies—A New Goal for Unions," *Monthly Labor Review,* June 1977, pp. 16–17.

18 Final Report, IUE Educational Advancement Program, 1969–1972, June 1, 1972.

19 *Employment and Training Report of the President,* 1977, p. 67.

20 *Employment and Training,* pp. 67–68.

21 Jonathan Grossman, *The Department of Labor,* New York: Praeger Publishers, 1973, p. 131.

22 William S. Franklin, "Journeyman Upgrading in Union Construction," *Industrial Relations,* October 1976, p. 322.

23 Ivan Charner et al., *An Untapped Resource: Negotiated Tuition-Aid in the Private Sector,* National Manpower Institute, Washington, D.C., 1978, p. 27.

24 Charner et al., p. 31.

25 The National Manpower Institute (now the National Institute for Work and Learning) has published a case study of the District 37 program entitled *The Education Fund of District Council 37: A Case Study.* Chapter 10 of this volume provides a fuller description of the District 37 program, based on the case study.

26 Herbert A. Levine, *Paid Educational Leave, NIE Papers in Education and Work,* No. 6, National Institute of Education, Washington, D.C., March 1977.

27 Carroll Hutton, "Paid Educational Leave in Canada," UAW Convention Report, April 1980.

28 Hazel P. Brown, "Labor Unions, Collective Bargaining and the Workplace," testimony before the U.S. Senate Labor and Human Resources Comitee, June 1979, p. 2. This testimony provides a complete description of the school and its operation.

29 Brown, p. 7.

30 Gus Tyler, "The University and the Labor Union: Educating the Proletariat," *Change*, February 1979, p. 36.

31 Tyler, pp. 62–63.

32 Levine and Fried, pp. 75–76.

33 Leonard Woodcock, "Education for a New Age: Partnership with Labor," *Community and Junior College Journal,* May 1975, p. 20.

34 Herbert Levine, "Will Labor Educators Meet Today's Challenges?," *Industrial Relations,* 1966, pp. 97–106.

35 Levine, "Will Labor Educators Meet Today's Challenges,?" *Industrial Relations,* 1966, pp. 97–106.

36 Gray, p. 16. This article lists all such institutions and the degrees they granted at that time. The number of community colleges offering the degree has grown since 1977.

37 The 1972 proposal is reprinted in Phyllis H. Isreal, *Education and Training Programs of the Operating Engineers Union,* Local Union No. 98, International Union of Operating Engineers, prepared for the National Institute of Education, June 1979.

38 William Abbott, "College/Labor Union Cooperation," *Community and Junior College Journal,* April 1977.

Chapter 8

In Colleges and Universities

The Congress finds that lifelong learning has a role in developing the potential of all persons including improvements of their personal well-being, upgrading their workplace skills, and preparing them to participate in the civic, cultural, and political life of the Nation.

Lifelong Learning Act of 1976

Throughout this complex and changing nation, there are now thousands of educational institutions in search of new learners, and there are millions of Americans in search of some fresh learning experience. But between those two quests and their respective goals stand a host of complexities that are often overlooked by enthusiasts for a prospective learning society, or they have triggered an excessive amount of skepticism and cynicism in the doubting Thomases.

George Bonham, *Change,* 1979

Higher education is approaching the territory of lifelong learning with standards, forethought, and a sense of dignity reminiscent of the California Gold Rush.

John C. Sawhill, *Change,* 1979

As we enter the 1980s, assessment of the prospects for adult learning in postsecondary education range from the wildly optimistic, to the cautiously encouraging, to the greatly troubled. The 1970s saw many colleges and universities rush headlong to serve adult populations, while many others reacted little, if at all. But the transformation was sufficiently widespread that a modern Rip Van Winkle, sleeping through the late 1960s and the 1970s, would have awakened to the sound of a new vocabulary that included experiential education, distance learning, off-campus learning, lifelong learning, recurrent education, competency-based instruction, open universities, and weekend colleges. No doubt, a few more terms will have been coined between the time this is written and the time it is read.

As a result of these developments, millions of working adults can now think realistically of combining education with work or of going back to school in order to go back to work. This beachhead of experience is sufficiently well grounded to constitute a firm base from which to plan an expansion of the beachhead's perimeter. Whether or not there are to be unacceptable casualties in terms of failed expectations, worthless credentials, or wasted public and private funds will depend on how good this plan is and whether the forces that have brought adult learning this far can regroup to tackle the "host of complexities" referred to by George Bonham.

To distinguish new adult students, new techniques of educating them, and new ways of granting credit, a label was created that heavily underscores the need to make the 1980s different from the late 1970s. This label is "nontraditional," used to characterize students, programs, and sometimes institutions or branches of institutions. It tells us what the modified subject is not, rather than what it is. It tells us that we no longer assume postsecondary institutions serve only the young in standard two- and four-year blocks of classroom time. But it does not tell us either what these institutions are or where they should be going. This label creates the same kind of discomfort as did the distinction between "whites and nonwhites" in government statistics until the late 1960s. This is more than just a deficiency of nomenclature; it is an indication that we have not yet achieved a system of adult education. Thus far, in many cases, we have merely tinkered with youth-serving institutions.

So the decade of the 1980s is a time for adult learning in colleges and universities to evolve beyond its status as an appendage to youth education. What is ventured in this chapter is no more than a taking stock, a preliminary to this large and important task. An accounting is made here of the scope of program development underway, of obstacles to greater adult opportunity, and of the limited assessments made of developments to date. Finally, several tentative steps are suggested for widening the perimeter.

A Showcase of New Approaches

Currently, there is little information about how many adults are engaged in each of the program approaches developed during the 1970s. The standard way of collecting statistics about postsecondary education does not reveal much about the changing nature of the adult education enterprise. We know, for example, how many students (of whatever age) are enrolled in engineering courses, but nothing about the level of enrollments in "weekend colleges," or how many degrees are awarded which give academic credit for life experiences that achieve college objectives. We need to become more systematic about measurement.

But we do know a lot about the *types* of program approaches and modifications of traditional practice taking place. There is now a showcase of new ways and means from which education institutions can elect to expand their services to adults. In some cases, our knowledge is adequate for making these choices. In other cases, it is not, and careful inspection is recommended. Major innovations of the last dozen or so years are described below.

One innovation easy to understand and visualize is the *weekend college* approach, by which the college serves youth during weekdays, and adults— particularly working adults—on Saturdays, Sundays, and sometimes Fridays. The weekend approach has the merit of fully utilizing existing facilities. One noteworthy example is the C. W. Post Center of Long Island University. Through this intensive system, adults can earn an associate, bachelor's, or master's degree.[1]

One of the best-known weekend colleges is at Wayne State University, started in 1973, granted authority to award a Bachelor of General Studies in 1974, and now enrolling over 3,000 students. One unique aspect of the Wayne State Weekend College is that it has "devised a means of recruiting and of teaching large numbers of blue-collar workers to bachelor's degree level."[2] The close relationship between Wayne State University and the United Automobile Workers figures large in this success.

The growth of the weekend college is not, however, confined to large universities. Liberal arts colleges are also reaching for adult students. One excellent example is the Weekend College, founded in 1977 at Hiram College in Ohio, which offers a B.A. degree. In order to make the college experience as complete as possible, students have the option of spending the weekend on the campus in special Weekend College Residence Halls. Enrollment is small—175 students—but so is Hiram, which has a regular enrollment of about 1,000. If all small liberal arts colleges offered programs of this kind, tremendous numbers of adults would be reached.

Instead of bringing adult students to the campus on weekends, *off-campus* programs bring the campus to the students. A striking example is Mercy College in New York City's northern suburbs. In ten years, this "faltering Catholic women's college with a $1 million budget and fewer than 1,000 students" was transformed into a $16-million enterprise offering coeducation to 8,500 students at six learning facilities.[3] Fifty-seven percent of the students are over 25 years old.

Off-campus learning is, however, the target for some of the strongest criticism leveled at nontraditional education for allegedly lowering educational standards. A 1979 story in the *Wall Street Journal* relates the transformation of Columbia College in Missouri from a small private college on the verge of collapse into a 3,000 part-time student operation in 144 off-campus locations.[4] Critics began charging the college with shortchanging students and sacrificing academic quality in the rush to enroll adults. After running into accreditation problems, tighter review was instituted and "Columbia College has agreed to reduce its off-campus locations from 144 to about 40 and to pare the number of adults enrolled by about two-thirds."

Institutions offering off-campus learning to adults counter that they are attacked partly because other schools fear their attractiveness to local students. Off-campus learning, it is argued, meets real needs by bringing education directly to working adults. In any case, off-campus learning is becoming a sizeable venture. Since 1971, approximately 150 colleges and universities have enrolled 60,000 adults in off-campus programs at subsidiaries established away from the regular university campuses.[5]

Innovations in adapting education practices to adults have overlapping applications. For example, off-campus programs established at subsidiaries away from the universities, in addition to providing classroom instruction, often award academic credit for life experience through what is known as the "assessment of experiential learning." The proposition is that much of what is learned through life and work experience merits and should receive academic credit. Therefore, adults going back to school should not have to do all classroom work for the standard two- or four-year program. The Commission on Non-Traditional Study, created in 1971, recommended sound assessment and credentialing practices. The Cooperative Assessment of Experiential Learning (CAEL) was established in 1974 to bring this about.[6]

Crediting for experience has become a common feature of adult education programs and CAEL (renamed the Council for Advancement of Experiential Learning) is now a consortium of about 100 colleges and universities. The debate over credit for experience is not so much about the principle as the specifics: how well credit is assessed, and how closely the experience is, or should be, related to the educational objectives of the institution. Even a strong critic of current practices in granting credit for experience, John Sawhill, then President of New York University, concluded that, "When adults can demonstrate that certain of their experiences are comparable to existing courses at an institution, the practice of awarding credit is appropriate and respectable."[7] This is not very different from the judgment expressed by this author in CAEL's younger days that "the problem must be kept clearly identified: it is assessing the degree to which a person, through experience, has achieved some of the educational goals of a particular institution."[8]

In addition to credit for prior experience, CAEL also advocates combined experience and classroom approaches. Its latest innovation, in the spring of

1980, is a new telephone service in which prospective learners can call to find out which of their local colleges or universities will provide credit for work or life experience.

In addition to grafts of nontraditional programs onto traditional institutions, there are emerging new, primarily adult institutions. One such institution, Kennedy University in California, calls itself "the first accredited upper-division and post-graduate institution in the country designed specifically for people in their mid-life passages." It has existed for 15 years. Kennedy has begun to offer full-fledged day programs as well as classes on nights and weekends. The goal is always to meet the needs of adult students, and this extends to arrangements for child care and to class schedules that enable a parent to be home before regular school is out. Kennedy's educational philosophy is encouraging at a time when much of adult education is reminiscent of an efficient cafeteria. As a dean at Kennedy says, "We look at education as a tapestry. There are lots of strands to education and to life. The real job comes not from pulling them apart, but from seeing how they weave together."[9]

There are new institutions that combine a number of the innovations of the 1970s. One of the best examples is Empire State College, a principal architect of the *external degree* in the United States. Derived from the British Open University and American correspondence programs, its external degree programs provide instruction with a minimum of time on the campus. A unique aspect of Empire State is that it was created for the express purpose of offering learning off campus. It combines "distance learning," "contract learning" (a contract between student and teacher), assessment of experience for academic credit, instruction and learning in work settings, and educational counseling.[10]

A quite different approach to distance learning is demonstrated by the University of Mid-America (UMA), a consortium of universities using multimedia techniques to bring higher education to off-campus students. UMA now reaches about 10,000 students through multimedia packages which combine television, print, newspapers, audio components, video discs, and satellite hookups. Degrees are awarded not by UMA, but by participating universities. Although media technology is the foundation for the enterprise, new technology at this point is not the problem, says UMA's President, Donald McNeil. "What institutions involved in nontraditional learning need at this point, especially from foundations and federal and state government, are monies to utilize the technology that's been developed; it's not the hardware that's needed; it's the software."[11]

There are also efforts to extend postsecondary vocational education to adults by reaching out beyond the confines of the school. One successful strategy, according to Gene Bottoms, Executive Director of the American Vocational Association, "has been *neighborhood outreach* centers that provide a variety of services—career counseling and planning, job orientation, financial assistance, job follow-through assistance—in addition to a program of vocational education."[12] An example of this strategy are the "Drop-In Centers" in six low-income neighborhoods in Kentucky that helped 3,500 men and women last year with homemaking skills. The centers are joint enterprises of the local boards of education and the Kentucky Bureau of Vocational Education.[13]

One of the largest vocational education outreach efforts is that of the Milwaukee Area Technical College (MATC), which served 105,000 part-time adults in 1977–78, and an additional 57,000 students, age 16 to 80, enrolled in regular daytime centers. Classes are held in industrial plants, schools, churches, social service agency offices, and jails. MATC has established close working relationships with industry in Milwaukee. According to the training director of the Harneschfeger Corporation, the training provided by MATC "is invaluable because we could not possibly provide the necessary instructional staff and facilities. MATC has helped hundreds of our employees advance and upgrade themselves, from the factory-type jobs up through supervisory, engineering, and technical positions."[14]

These are but a few of the more significant items in the showcase of nontraditional postsecondary education. Educational institutions with an interest in adults will find many other examples, requiring close inspection and careful choices.

How Has Education Changed?

It is easy to describe a few examples of innovations, and to spot the more visible and respected edifices on the landscape of nontraditional learning. But what do we know about how *much* change there is in higher education, and what its results are? Are significant numbers of adults reached? Are their objectives met? These are important questions, to which there are as yet few answers. But fragments of information here and there provide hints. A few quantitative statements can be made about the developments of the 1970s which may help in framing future questions.

One of those quantitative statements, and the one most striking of all, is about the role that community and junior colleges have played in spearheading the development of learning opportunity for adults. The enrollment of part-time students in these colleges reached 2.7 million in 1979, up .4 million from just four years earlier. There is growth, to be sure, in other places, but this remarkable statistic underscores the extent to which these two-year colleges are critical in the worklife learning scene.

To summarize, modifications introduced by two-year colleges to accommodate adults include

1. scheduling classes at times other than during the morning or afternoon, when the majority of adults are at work. More classes are being held at night or on weekends, and more institutions have "weekend colleges."

2. offering classes at locations other than the main campus. Courses are being given at regional campus centers as well as libraries, employment sites, union halls, churches, and even on commuter trains.

3. awarding academic credit for life and work experiences.

4. using the media to transmit courses, lectures, and reading materials. A number of courses are being given through local newspapers; others are shown on cable TV several times during the week. Lectures are taped on television so that students may come in and view the tapes at times convenient to their schedules.

5. easing admissions requirements and formal entry qualifications for certain courses of study.

6. encouraging greater use of independent study, which may be more challenging and appropriate to the needs of adult learners.

Despite the fact that the great majority of colleges and universities still expect their adult students to enroll in regular academic programs, there has been marked growth in the development of nontraditional programs in colleges and universities over the last decade.[15] In a study conducted for the Commission on Non-Traditional Study in 1972, Ruyle and Geiselman found that:

- Students in three out of four American colleges and universities can earn undergraduate degrees entirely on a part-time basis. (The figure for public community colleges is nine out of ten—more than for any other type of institution.)

- Part-time students are eligible for some financial aid in more than half of the schools that allow them to earn degrees entirely on a part-time basis, but one-third of the schools have no financial aid for part-time students.

- Separate counseling and advisement services for adults are offered in less than 10 percent of the schools surveyed.

- Of the programs designed for nontraditional students, over half are for housewives and working adults, while 48 percent are aimed at special occupational groups, such as health workers or government employees.

- Sixty-two percent of the programs include occupational and career preparation in the curriculum. Most of the occupational preparation programs are off-campus courses of short duration which lead to a certificate or to an associate or graduate degree.

- Nearly two out of three programs use some form of technological teaching aid, such as tape cassettes, programmed instruction, videotapes, and talkback TV.

It would be useful to bring this study up to date, since nontraditional forms and offerings have undoubtedly diversified. Despite the study's statement that "there is something for everyone somewhere in the accredited colleges and universities across the United States," Ruyle and Geiselman conclude with the disturbing observation that

> in many institutions that claim to welcome the part-time or adult student, the special needs of these potential students are not being met—needs for lower fees, special counselors, counseling, financial aids, business and job placement, offices open at times when the student is on campus, child care, grants, work-study jobs. More community colleges than other institutions try to provide for the needs of part-time and adult students.[16]

To the best of our knowledge, there are no comprehensive directories of nontraditional programs and practices for adults in the United States. We do know that nontraditional learning opportunities include a broad spectrum of activities at the postsecondary level. Some of these options open to adult learners include

independent study (full-time/part-time)

three-year B.A. degree

individual learning contracts

external degrees

internships/work-study programs

correspondence or home study courses

tutorial study courses

televised instruction

computer-assisted instruction

cassette-based courses

In addition, credit may be granted for such diverse experiences as learning in proprietary schools

learning in industrial/in-service training programs

study abroad

learning in community-based groups

volunteer work

employment experience

artistic achievement

military service

learning in the military

Other services which may be offered to adult learners include

special counseling for adults

child care services

credit by examination without course enrollment requirements

admission for adults over the age of 25 without a high school diploma or equivalency certificate

Our information can sustain only a few comments about the suitability of a few of these arrangements to meet the learning needs of adults.

One of the most frequently cited forms of nontraditional postsecondary education for adults is the external degree program, discussed earlier. Cyril Houle defines the external degree as "one awarded to an individual on the basis of some program preparation (devised either by himself or by an educational institution) which is not centered on traditional patterns of residential collegiate or university study."[17] He goes on to differentiate further among three types of external degrees—the extension, the adult, and the third-generation external degree.

The extension degree . . . is one awarded on completion of a coherent and complete traditional degree program . . . at a time or place accessible to those who cannot come to the campus or whose other responsibilities make it necessary for them to spread their study over a longer period than does the student on campus. In admission, instruction, evaluation, and certification, few or no changes are made.

The adult degree . . . was developed in the belief that adults . . . are so different from young people that a program of studies designed for men and women should be based at every point on their maturity. Such a degree may depart completely from traditional patterns . . . or it may mix new elements with old ones.

The third-generation external degree, emphasizing assessment and demonstration of competence, is developing on the basis that one or more of the traditional procedures of higher education—admission, teaching, evaluation, certification, or licensure—can be so modified or separated from the others that the actual learning of the student, rather than his completion of formal requirements, can become the center of attention and the basis of the awarding of the degree.[18]

An example of the third-generation external degree program is the New York Regents External Degree, which requires only that the student prepare for (in any way he or she chooses) and successfully pass a set of examinations. People from the ages of 19 to 74 have participated in this program across the country. More than 85 percent of the participants are employed on a full-time basis, the majority serving in the military or as nurses; others are teachers, business people, police, and homemakers. Currently, 12,000 are working toward a Regents External Degree; 5,000 have already graduated. The cost of obtaining the degree varies, depending on how the necessary credits are earned; if they are earned entirely by examination, costs range from $400 to $850.[19] According to Houle, "this program breaks profoundly with the past so far as every major procedural point is concerned," that is, there are no formal admissions requirements. All effective methods of learning are acceptable and accomplishment is measured by a variety of methods.[20]

Many external degree programs have patterned themselves closely after Great Britain's successful Open University model, which combines seminars, TV and radio instruction, and correspondence material. At Empire State College, established by the State University of New York in 1971, students and faculty design individualized programs, working closely under learning contracts with regular faculty members or faculty from other institutions, and with tutors affiliated with one of Empire State's 36 learning centers, units, and locations across New York State. As of March 1979, over 5,000 students had graduated from the College, and the total enrollment of full- and part-time students was 3,200. Empire State has developed the Center for Distance Learning for those students desiring more structure than that offered by learning contracts, and who cannot or prefer not to attend classes. Structured degree programs are made available through the Center, using educational materials that have been specifically designed for those who will be "learning at a distance." Study materials developed by the British Open University have been adapted and offered to small groups who also have regular access to supplementary study materials and to a tutor on a twice-weekly group study basis.

Currently, cooperative arrangements are being developed within the State University and with other institutions in hopes of increasing the range of courses and degree programs offered through the Center for Distance Learning.[21]

In a 1977 study designed to learn more about external degree programs and about the characteristics and experiences of degree holders, the Bureau of Social Science Research identified 244 external degree programs in 134 colleges and universities. In 1976, these programs enrolled approximately 54,000 students; since their founding (usually after 1972), 4,600 A.A. and 14,000 B.A. degrees have been granted. A survey of 1,500 degree recipients provided the following data, indicating students with basically traditional interests and aims:

- The B.A. graduates were predominately white, male, thirty to forty years old, married, and working in professional or subprofessional occupations.

- Four out of five students had been enrolled previously in a traditional degree program.

- In response to the question of why they chose an external degree program rather than a traditional one, most of the respondents mentioned the chance to receive credit for all prior college course work, the ability to maintain a regular work schedule, flexible scheduling, and part-time study opportunities.

- Graduates placed low value on being able to convert life or work experience into academic credits.

- With regard to motivation, the satisfaction of having a degree was the highest-ranked goal. Job-related benefits and the opportunity to gain access to further education were equally rated secondary motivations for external degree seekers.

In sum, the study concluded that, contrary to what many people believed, external degree programs were used mainly by traditionally oriented degree seekers rather than previously unserved students. These programs represent only a

> tiny segment of a huge degree-granting enterprise; they seem to serve extremely well a very special group of degree seekers who cannot be accommodated by traditional considerations designed for a younger student population. In fact, these programs admirably serve the needs of an older, well-prepared clientele.[22]

The University of Mid-America (UMA), described earlier, uses television to broadcast courses into the homes of 4,000 students located in a multistate region of the Midwest, and is reaching quite a different audience from that described by the Bureau of Social Science Research. In 1977, thirteen courses were offered in Nebraska alone to students ranging in age from 9 to 87, averaging 37. There are no admission requirements; nearly half of UMA's students have never attended college before. Approximately 75 percent of the participants are women, most of whom are enrolled for credit. More than a third of the students live in rural areas or remote small towns. For these learners, UMA often represents the only opportunity to work toward a college degree.[23]

The University Without Walls (UWW), formally initiated in 1971, calls itself "an alternative form of higher education," a "highly individualized form of undergraduate education, which abandons the sharply circumscribed campus and provides for independent self-directed study and work experience."[24] UWW is a national network of nearly thirty U.S. colleges and universities that have instituted UWW programs at their schools. In 1975, some 6,000 students, ranging in age from 16 to 70, were enrolled in individually planned programs to obtain degrees based mainly on off-campus learning and independent study. Admissions policies vary among individual schools from liberal to highly selective, but once admitted each student follows a tailor-made program designed by the student and her/his adviser. Students have access to a variety of learning modes: regular courses, field experiences, independent study, individual and group projects, travel, and technological aids. Because there is no prescribed curriculum or uniform time schedule, graduation takes place when the student has achieved the learning objectives agreed upon in designing his/her program of study.[25]

It is probably too early to assess the impact all these changes are having on adult learning and its relationship to worklife needs. This has been a period of creation, rather than of sifting and assessment. But enough is now in place to examine seriously both the quality of programs and the degree to which these changes match the needs of working adults. There is, of course, a general awareness that the rush to sign up the adult student has created some crassness, shortchanging of students, and false advertising. It is enough to cause some educators to blush, but not at all enough to sustain any general charges against the changes of the 1970s.

Equal Treatment?

The largest impediment to equal service in higher education for adult workers is plain prejudice—prejudice against the adult learner.

It is not as if American education is without a tradition of teaching the adult.

Our past includes the lyceum lectures and the Chautauquas. William Rainey Harper made home study a part of the founding of the University of Chicago in the 1890s. And Charles R. Van Hise, President of the University of Wisconsin after its 1907 reorganization, said: "I shall never rest content until the beneficient influence of the University . . . shall be made available in every home in the state."[26]

However, most institutions came to identify education with the young, and in too many instances still do, despite earlier traditions and despite the favorable experience of the GI Bill. An interview with a university administrator in 1973 provoked the comment about adult students that "few of them have a genuine intellectual interest. They want a degree for career advancement, or come because they are bored. Every reason except to get educated. When bachelors and bachelor girls write to the lonesome columns, the Aid-to-the-Lovelorn twins say 'If you're looking for company or for a mate, join a church or take an adult education course.' "[27]

Fred Harvey Harrington, in his *The Future of Adult Education,* sums it up:

> Most colleges and universities are still unwilling to place the training of adults in the teaching basket where it belongs. Rather they toss it into the catch-all public service function of higher education, along with such important but academically low-priority activities as fund raising and alumni, legislative, and community relations. In budgetary terms, this means unsatisfactory financing in the best of times, the axe in tight periods.[28]

This view of the adult education enterprise is commonly held, of course, outside the colleges and universities. It is embedded in public education law, for example. Although 12 years of publicly paid education is a matter of right (13 years including kindergarten, 14 with a Headstart program), this social contract contains some significant fine print: you must be young. The majority of state statutes prescribe both lower and upper age limits for enrollment in the public school system. A check on 1974 laws showed little change since a compilation of state requirements in 1966. The situation then was outlined below, with a number of special conditions and exceptions not summarized.[29]

Number of States	Maximum Age of Public School Attendance
26	21 years
4	20 years
1	19 years
3	18 years
18	Not specified in statute

A 40-year-old who left school at the end of the tenth grade does not have his or her two years of education stored safely in the bank, an amount equal to about $3,000 at today's costs of public education. One large step toward making adult education financially feasible for more adults would be to make the 12 years of public education an entitlement that extends throughout life, so that those who now have the least education would have better access to it.[30]

But the principal point of reviewing these laws is that they embody the view that public education is principally for the young, and the extent to which this view has permeated society. To be sure, this view is changing, but a great many of the specific difficulties for adult learning have their roots in this general attitude.

It is this attitude that resulted in the limitations placed on student financial aid. A striking example is New York State, where even though part-time students (mostly adults) represent 30 percent of all undergraduates, they received "less than 6 percent of the $529 million in federal student aid and only about 10 percent of $206 million in state aid."[31] When the United States gets really serious about the need for education and training throughout working life, as well as during youth, it will attend to these issues of financial aid, and to education entitlements during the adult years.[32]

While there have been some changes in federal financial aid laws, a number of restrictions remain that put adults in a status quite unequal to youth:[33]

- Prohibitions against less than half-time enrollment. This prohibition exists in all six federal student aid programs, and limits the ability of many working adults to take advantage of student aid.

- Aid for undergraduate study only. The restriction to undergraduates of three aid programs (BEOG, SEOG, SSIG) makes it more difficult to use education and training as a means of shifting occupations when necessitated by technological change and market forces.

- Restriction to degree or certificate programs. This restriction excludes adults who want refresher courses, weekend colleges, new forms of experimental learning opportunities, or very specific skill courses. A complete removal of the restriction would be very costly, but a review could be made to see if a fair line could be drawn.

- Unequal student contributions. The "independent" applicant to the BEOG program is expected to contribute more to his or her own support than parents are expected to contribute to the support of a dependent. While this is not a simple issue, a close review is merited to eliminate unequal treatment as much as possible.

- "Proration" of awards. A less than full-time student has his or her BEOG award "reduced in proportion to the degree the student is not so attending on a full-time basis." The hours groupings used for applying this rule work to the disadvantage of many students by giving them less than a straight proportional reduction would.

- The minimum award. The current minimum award in BEOG and SEOG of $200 precludes many adult students from going to school part-time, and requires them to prove "exceptional circumstances" to get less than $200.

- Time limitations. The typical four-year limitation on achieving an educational objective was set with the full-time student in mind. This needs to be changed to recognize that the part-time student needs more time to reach the same objective.

While these restrictions affect many adults, they fall particularly hard on older women, as is pointed out by Robert Sexton:

> Women are most likely to be part-time students and more often than not over 35 years old when they attend school. They are also more likely to need financial aid. There is a need for special provisions for older women with children; they need aid for child care expenses, and need good financial aid information since they may not be able to participate in the normal information channels.[34]

There are, to be sure, costs associated with more equal treatment in awarding financial aid. These have to be assessed and changes made step by step, based on what we can collectively afford. And the benefits—ranging from increased earning power to enlarged tax receipts to a more knowledgeable democratic citizenry—also need to be taken into account when budget problems are contemplated.

A New Tradition

It is time to get rid of all the "nons" that are affixed to the education and training of adults. Terms such as nontraditional education, nontraditional students, and nondependents are a good place to start. But there now is a showcase of experience from which to choose and combine options. To step into a different kind of future means being just as sure about what this new learning is as what it is not. There needs to be a new understanding of adult learning defined not simply by its contrast to the old traditions.

This means developing a philosophy of education and defining its purposes. More precisely, it means developing a considerable number of philosophies and purposes. For we have every reason to expect a diversity of philosophies among practitioners of the new learning, as there are among postsecondary educators of youth.

Our apprehension is not occasioned by the prospect of many philosophies and purposes, but rather by the possibility that many institutions will have neither. Educational institutions that have a philosophy of education for youth are not excused from having one for adults. What does it mean to educate people while they are living their adult lives and after they have had many life experiences, in contrast to equipping youth to become adults? We suspect that careful reflection and thought will suggest that there are differences, and there are similarities. Many institutions will emphasize differences rather than similarities. But others, we suspect, will see little difference in terms of their institutions' missions. This seems somewhat the case with the Weekend College at Hiram College, whose brochure invites adults to look at the regular catalogue of offerings, eat in the dining rooms, live (for the weekend) in the dormitories, and go to the student activities.

From clear thinking about the purposes of adult education will come standards of good quality. It is difficult to think clearly when there are so many battles to fight over changing standards designed for youth to make education possible for adults. But standards are no less essential because existing ones do not apply. It is particularly important that the matter of standards be given high priority as we enter a period of temptation when institutions will have too few students to sustain them, or too few to sustain as large a staff and plant as in the past. Thinking through a philosophy of educating adults, and defining institutional purpose, is well worth the time of the trustees of educational institutions. There is good reason to fear that this thinking is being done in too few places.

Related to standards and philosophy is the question of balance between responsiveness and responsibility. Educators do need to find out what workers want, and what employers want workers to know, and it is responsible to do so. But adults and workers also should expect the institutions themselves to make judgments about what an education ought to be and to state these judgments clearly so that adults can choose thoughtfully among institutions.

Recently, an employer at a major conference on the interrelation of community colleges and industry said that "because of current and future funding problems for community colleges, the institutions may find it wise to limit their curricula and specialization for their students and customers—business and industry."[35] It is responsive for community colleges to make sure the occupational training they offer is recognized and utilized by a community's employers. But it does not meet the test of responsibility to the working adult to be solely responsive to industry skill needs. Education institutions need to know what they are about when any interest group tries to stake out a claim.

The matter of standards and quality will become more pressing as the hardware of communications technology becomes more accessible for educational ventures. Excitement is caused inevitably by the wonders of the technology itself. But the development of content requires long lead time and good minds, and it seldom receives the necessary attention. The effort (such as that by the University of Mid-America) to keep content at least up to par with · technology may be the most important item now on the agenda for adult learning.

All of the matters of equity affecting education throughout working life require attention in the 1980s. This certainly includes the status of the part-time learner in federal and other student financial aid programs.

* * * *

The most exciting and far-reaching change in American education in quite some time has been the opening of postsecondary education to the adult learner and full-time worker. It has momentum and it has energy. It has leaders who have cleared new paths, invented new approaches, and fought the necessary battles' with the forces of inertia and indifference. What remains is the challenge of finishing the job, and getting in place a new tradition in which adults are so much a part of the college and university scene that their presence there is unremarkable.

Notes

1   Victor Meskill, *Learner Centered Reform,* p. 107, cited in Martin Carry, "Learner Needs, Federal Policy, and Nontraditional Postsecondary Education: A Convergence of Interests," August 1978, unpublished.

2   P. Bertelsen, P. Fordham, and J. London, "Evaluation of the Wayne State University's University Studies and Week-end College Programme," UNESCO, 1977, p. 5.

3   George Bonham, "Inching Toward the Learning Society," *Change,* July-August 1979, p. 57.

4   Andy Pasztor and Rich Jaroslovsky, "Question of Degree: Colleges Find Dollars in Branches for Adults, but Some Lose Quality," *Wall Street Journal,* May 21, 1979.

5   Pasztor and Jaroslovsky.

6   Morris Keeton, *Experiential Learning: Rationale, Characteristics, and Assessment,* San Francisco: Jossey-Bass, 1976, p. xvi. This book remains a useful compendium of theory and practice, although use of these techniques has become more widespread since 1976.

7   John Sawhill, "Lifelong Learning: Scandal of the Next Decade?," *Change,* December–January 1978–79.

8   Paul Barton, "Learning Through Work and Education," in Keeton, p. 128.

9   William Sievert, "A California Campus Where Adults Can Return to College on Their Own Terms," *Chronicle of Higher Education,* December 12, 1977.

10 For a good description of how various nontraditional programs combine a number of different approaches, see Martin Carry, p. 27.

11 Karin Abarbanel, "University of Mid-America: Reaching the Long Distance Learner, *Foundation News,* May–June 1979, p. 8.

12 Gene Bottoms, "Adults—An Underdeveloped National Resource," *Voc Ed,* November 1978, p. 12.

13 "It Works," *Voc Ed,* November 1978, p. 26.

14 Don Rich, "Milwaukee Reaches Out to Its Adults," *Voc Ed,* November 1978, p. 26.

15 Janet Ruyle and Lucy Ann Geiselman, "Non-Traditional Opportunities and Programs," in *Planning Non-Traditional Programs,* Patricia Cross and John Valley, San Francisco: Jossey-Bass, 1974.

16 Ruyle and Geiselman, p. 91.

17 Cyril Houle, *The External Degree,* San Francisco: Jossey-Bass, 1973, p. 9.

18 Houle, pp. 88–90.

19 Ronald Gross, *The Lifelong Learner,* New York: Simon and Schuster, 1977, pp. 16–17.

20 Houle, p. 97.

21 The British Open University Foundation, Inc., "An Occasional Newsletter," No. 4, March 1979, pp. 1–3.

22 Laura Sharp, "Viewpoint—External Degrees: Myths and Realities," *Change,* July–August 1979, p. 70.

23 Ronald Gross, *New Paths to Learning: College Education for Adults,* Public Affairs Committee, New York, 1977, pp. 11–12.

24 UECU Press Release, p. 2.

25 *University Without Walls: First Report,* 1972, p. 4.

26 Fred Harvey Harrington, *The Future of Adult Education,* San Francisco: Jossey-Bass, 1977, pp. 10–18. Harrington provides a history (in chapter 2) of the tradition in higher education with respect to adults.

27 Harrington, p. 7.

28 Harrington, p. 8.

29 August Steinhilber and Carl Sokolowski, "State Law on Compulsory Attendance," U.S. Office of Education, Washington, D.C., 1966.

30 For a fuller description of this proposal, see Paul E. Barton, "Lifelong Learning: Getting Started," *Chicago School Review,* May 1978, pp. 319–322.

31 Robert Purga, "Financial Aid and the Adult Learner: Federal and New York State Student Aid Programs," unpublished paper prepared for the State Education Department, Albany, New York, January 24, 1979.

32 For examination of these issues and prospects, see particularly Purga; Norman Kurland, ed., *Entitlement Studies,* National Institute of Education, 1977; and Douglas Windham, Norman Kurland, and Florence Levinsohn, "Financing the Learning Society," *Chicago School Review,* May 1978.

33 For a fuller treatment, see Robert F. Sexton, *Barriers to the Older Student: The Limits of Federal Financial Aid Benefits,* National Institute for Work and Learning (formerly National Manpower Institute), 1980.

34 Sexton, p. 12.

35 Craig Musick, "What Employees Need in Training and How to Promote Cooperation Between ASTD and AACJC and AVA," paper presented at Wingspread Conference Center, Racine, Wisconsin, March 12–14, 1980.

Chapter 9

Later Worklife

I never realized that my work career, title, status, job responsibilities, office, secretary, even desk represented my turf, or territory, and thus largely defined my identify to others and to myself. . . . It was only at retirement, when all aspects of my turf were given to another, that the dreadful realization of being turfless struck home. For an awful moment, I became uncertain of my identity. I knew who I had been, but I was not certain who I was.

Leland P. Bradford, retired in 1970

To build a code of conduct toward the old requires not only personal kindliness but generations of the practice of values from which the old are not excluded—of which indeed they are the summation.

Max Lerner, America as a Civilization, 1957

They deal with age as if it were a birthmark instead of a birthday.

Ellen Goodman, 1980

The survey asked me if I was retired. Retired from what, I would like to know.

Dot Kern, 60-year-old housewife, Lumberton, North Carolina

The most striking paradox of American working life has to do with the value placed on experience in the workplace. For the young job seeker and advancing worker, experience is a valued commodity, hard to get enough of. For workers staring into the sixth decade of life, with the most experience of all, hanging on in the employment world becomes very hard, and more and more slip quietly into a state of life called "retirement."

Nothing in American society is more perplexing than what we think of and how we handle the process of growing older. Ambiguities and paradoxes abound and are, of course, not limited to workplaces. In a society that still places high value on the characteristics of youth, older people are complimented for "not looking their age," while in other societies reverence increases with age. Greater affluence, among young and old, has resulted in an increasing poverty of emotional support as that affluence permits the "nuclear family" and older people live by themselves. The view is nurtured that retirement is the reward for a long worklife, but facing it often triggers the largest of life's anxieties. Employers short on managerial and technical skills often force out people who have those skills under mandatory retirement policies. Folk wisdom has it that you are never too old to learn, but few classrooms have welcome mats out for those who would seem to qualify the most.

Life is a seamless web, and it is a very large proposition to build a new code of conduct toward the old, particularly from the narrow perspective of working life and the education and training related to it. But embedded in worklife (in the broad sense of productive activity in general) is a large measure of the purpose that sustains life in its later years, when mating, child rearing, and work establishment have been left behind. So it is the proposition of this chapter that an improved relation among work, education, and training in life's later years is an effective opening wedge in revaluing American seniors in a society where being young has had the highest value of all.

Through this small window we will view a distant landscape where could grow a "practice of values where the old are not excluded," where the Leland Bradfords know who they are as well as who they have been and where the Dot Kerns are as rewarded and recognized for their careers as are those paid salaries and wages for a nine-to-five workday.

Convenient Misconceptions

It is not as clear as it should be how attitudes about when a person should stop working were shaped over the decades. There has developed a rather wide consensus, or at least practice, that age 65 is a normal retirement age. Both workers and employers have come to accept it, and it's pretty hard to sort out how much worker expectation is based on employer practice and how much workers really want to stay in employment beyond that age. The practice of "early retirement," which has been encouraged to varying degrees by corporations, unions, and the Social Security system, is coming to mean any time before age 65 (62 under the Social Security system and various ages in unilateral and collectively bargained pension plans).

The most plausible explanation for our current concept of retirement age is that the idea of retirement developed when work was mainly physical labor, whether on the farm or in the foundry, and the expected life span was shorter. On the farm, people worked about as long as they lived because they had to, and the body began to wear out at around the age of 65. After work could be performed no more, security was mainly achieved through children, and in the urban factory even that slipped away as the extended family gradually gave way to the nuclear one. Retirement policy is a surprisingly recent development for most workers, although it began with Social Security over 50 years ago. According to Roger O'Meara, "Recent years have seen the coming of a retirement revolution. The nation's wage and salary earners, who only a generation ago had to stay on their careers until they died or were disabled, now have to retire on reaching an appointed age—usually 65."[1] In the United States, the breakthrough in allowing people to live without working began in 1935 with the passage of the Social Security Act, although it was a long time after that before even bare subsistence was possible solely through Social Security payments. (The Act provided both for social insurance and old age assistance. The original intent of Social Security was to supplement income and not to be adequate by itself.) Age 65 was chosen as the retirement age under that legislation. It was a major advance in American civilization when a floor was put under income for the aging population.

As the idea of a floor under financial security evolved for those no longer able to work, the nature of work changed for the great majority of people. The change was to the point where work, for most of the working population, no longer involved physically strenuous labor, such as farming, digging ditches, lifting heavy objects. Over this period, assumptions about retirement changed in a surprising way: though work was getting physically easier, people began to retire earlier. This happened for more than one reason, including the increasing possibility of financial independence, new attitudes about how rewarding the job is as a part of life, and the needs of employers to reduce workforces as technology either reduced labor requirements in particular industries or changed the skills to the point where it was the older workers who would either have to be retrained or retired. Workforce adjustments through earlier retirement, whether induced through financial incentives or required, appeared to many to be the less painful way to go, allegedly creating more opportunities at the bottom for younger workers and "breadwinners."

While considerations about appropriate retirement age go well beyond a simple determination of the age at which employees become physically unable to work, the question of when that time arises remains a central one. The difficulty of answering that question on a case-by-case basis in large organizations is what has led to uniform and mandatory retirement policies. A single rule avoids an individual-by-individual determination, which is never easy and is very hard to back up with data.

Employers, of course, would claim that the age chosen is an average based on their actual experience with productive ability. But to our knowledge actual measurement to see how older workers perform individually and collectively is a rarity, and only a few studies can claim precision and objectivity. It is a bit hard to understand the underlying basis for retirement policy, in terms of worker ability, when such policies have emerged as work has become physically *easier* and when there have been so few studies of the relationship between age and the ability to perform at work.

What few studies there have been have mainly questioned whether older workers perform less well or substantially less well than younger ones. A study conducted from 1955 to 1957 in the footwear and household furniture industries indicated that productivity decreased slightly after age 45 and only somewhat more significantly after age 65. Some physical effort is required in such work. A study of office workers from 1958 to 1959 found that those aged 65 and over maintained the best results, with accuracy and output equal to that of younger workers and with greater consistency of output. A study made in 1961 of mail sorters investigated the relationship of consistency of output to experience on the job and found that the index of consistency rose with each advancing seniority group.[2] Other studies of age and work performance suggest that all dimensions of a job have to be examined, including past experience, stability, and maturity as well as the physical requirements of the job.[3]

These studies are limited and out-of-date, but they are solid enough to question assumptions regarding decline in productivity as a solid and accurate basis for mandatory retirement policy. At least, they make a strong case for finding out more about the relationship between age and industrial performance. And if what we are talking about is not performance but best ways of allocating scarce jobs among competing groups in the labor force, that issue might be better met head on and resolved in ways that do not tell older workers that they are no longer productive citizens.

This chapter is about the role of education and training in worklife adjustments of older workers and those who would otherwise be retirees. But the first question is whether the choice of an extended worklife is possible. If not, there is no role for education and training to play, from an occupational adjustment standpoint. Limited knowledge suggests that age alone is not a detriment to pursuing worklife after age 60, or 62, or 65, or 70, or more. But it is also conceded that surprisingly little solid information exists in industry on the relation of age to productive capacity.

Inconvenient Facts

If retirement has gotten earlier as work has become less physically demanding, it is also true that worklife for men has been shortening as life itself has been lengthening. On the one hand, the trends of the last twenty years are for earlier retirement. On the other, breakthroughs in medicine, and the broadening of opportunity for health care, have increased life expectancy. The result is that the period of *not working* has been growing steadily. The picture for women in this regard is not as clear because more women are now working longer than they used to, so as those with careers similar to men are affected by the same retirement policies, the total number of years women work has been lengthening. The Department of Labor estimates work and life expectancy as follows:

	Life and Work Expectancy at Birth		
	1900	1950	1970
MEN			
Life expectancy	48.2	65.5	67.1
Work expectancy	32.1	41.5	40.0
Nonwork expectancy	16.1	24.0	27.0
WOMEN			
Life expectancy	50.7	71.0	74.8
Work expectancy	6.3	15.1	22.9
Nonwork expectancy	44.4	55.9	51.9

Source: Bureau of Labor Statistics, Special Labor Force Report No. 187, 1977

A look at these trends is a reminder that the patterns of working life differ for men and women, that fewer women have had the kind of access to the job market that brings them face to face with retirement policies, and that those women who do work full lives and are now reaching retirement age are likely to be concentrated in industries and occupations where private retirement systems are either nonexistent or offer minimal benefits.

For men, worklife expectancy has been going down, and when the estimates are made for 1980 they will likely show that there are now nearly 30 years when men do not work. The expectancies for nonwork become very similar in terms of sex if we look at people in the labor force at a particular age. For those in the labor force at age 50, the worklife expectancy for men in 1970 was 14.8 years, compared with 15.0 years for single women, 12.0 years for married women without children, and 13.6 years for women divorced, widowed, or separated. But because women live longer than men, the years of nonworking life are substantially more: 8.4 years for 50-year-old working men compared to 13.9 years for 50-year-old single, working women.

There is a growing period of time, as a result of these trends, when people have to be supported with public and private pensions. What this means is that the nonwork option is getting increasingly costly to both employers and tax-payers. On the public side, everyone who works is aware of the financial problems of the Social Security system as paychecks have larger and larger deductions for payroll taxes. On the private side, federal pension plan oversight and collective bargaining have been forces to liberalize pension plan features (particularly with respect to vesting) at the same time that retirees see dimin-ishing support in real terms due to the erosion caused by inflation. For a number of reasons, the economics which have developed suggest that it costs to keep workers on the payroll longer and that these costs merit even offering financial incentives for early retirement. The question for careful investigation is whether some combination of longer lives, liberalized public and private retirement benefits, and unchecked inflation (at least as this is written in 1981) has altered these economics.

From the worker side of the equation, the economics are making it harder and harder to opt for early retirement. Inflation has hit people on fixed incomes very hard. Continued working will become increasingly attractive to the extent that double-digit inflation remains a part of the American economic landscape.

Overlaid on these economic and personal considerations is the fact that, for reasons of both longevity and demography, an increasing proportion of our population is over 65. A smaller proportion of the population will be support-ing the older population, and as Social Security taxes rise even more in these inflationary times, we may see a new kind of generation gap in which such support breeds resentment. From 1950 to 1980, the population age 25 to 64 grew by about 40 percent while the population age 65 and over nearly doubled. The growth of the over-65 age group will continue throughout the 1980s, until the dip in births which began in the Great Depression begins to slow the increase. That respite will be short-lived, however, as the World War II baby boom bursts into its sixth decade shortly after the year 2000. Twenty years is not very long to change practices and attitudes developed over many decades and even centuries. It is hard to imagine the protesters of the 1960s being as quiescent about denied work rules and eroded retirement incomes as their parents are in 1980.

In the face of these facts, is there a basis in both institutional and personal economics to examine closely the premises and practices that have led to earlier retirement over the last 20 or so years?

A First Shot?

A large question as we enter the decade of the 1980s is whether the law passed in 1978 raising the permissible mandatory retirement age from 65 to 70 is a first shot in a revolt against both the trend and requirement for retirement at age 65 (or earlier) or just a misfire. The law clearly prevents mandatory retirement until age 70, but opinion is quite divided as to whether it will change the actual retirement trends. If workers continue to be offered earlier retirement, will they take it in the future as they have in the past? How easily will employers adapt to the new policies? Are the economics changing so that employers will actually encourage workers to stay around longer? Was this new law the result of strong political forces coming from the grass roots or simply the result of very effective leadership in the Congress, passed because some of our most effective leaders were well beyond age 65?

A careful look at the recent data suggests that perhaps something has begun to happen in the labor force that is different from what has been going on for several decades. The decline in labor force participation rates among those over age 55 has generally slowed or halted altogether, and in one case it even reversed for the first time. The decline continues among males age 55 to 64, but while it had been dropping about a percentage point a year from 1966 to 1976, the participation rate dropped only from 74.5 percent in 1976 to 73.0 percent in 1979, or about half a point a year. Among males 65 and over, the rate has not been declining, with the 1976 rate of 20.3 percent changing only to 20.0 percent by 1979.

After being in decline from 1967 to 1974, the participation rate of women age 55 to 64 has been rising slightly, from 40.8 percent in 1976 to 41.9 percent in 1979, and for women 65 and over, the rate stabilized at 8.0 percent after dropping from 10.6 percent in 1960 to 8.0 percent in 1974.[4]

There is another factor that could be involved in moderating declining participation in the labor force among older workers. There is a considerable differential in labor force participation rates, at identical age levels, by educational attainment. For example, in 1978, men 65 and over with one to three years of high school had participation rates of 20 percent, compared with 32 percent for those with four or more years of college.[5] As the average educational attainment of the older labor force advances, there should be greater labor force participation from that factor alone. It is also the case that the participation rates of those with college educations have dropped less than the rates for those with only high school educations.

The desire to extend worklives beyond "normal" retirement ages is, in any event, not summed up in the labor force participation rates. Older persons give up looking for work after testing the market and finding that no one appears willing to hire them. According to a recent study based on ten years of labor force data beginning in 1968, approximately 23 percent of people over age 60 are appropriately classified as discouraged workers, meaning that they want work but are not currently looking for work and thus not included in the count of the labor force.[6] And the status of retirement policy in large firms with retirement plans, where workers have made careers, does not tell the whole story of employment opportunity for older workers. To a considerable extent, opportunities will have to be looked for in other firms, in part-time job opportunities, and in "second careers," or in retraining for different jobs where shortages exist in the firms from which older workers would otherwise be retired. Hints of a strengthened desire for employment come from a recent Lou Harris survey indicating that more workers than expected may postpone retirement, because of economic and social changes.[7]

The statistics collected by the Bureau of Labor Statistics establish that there are significant numbers of older persons not working who would like to work, even beyond those counted as unemployed. If they perceived the opportunities to be there, they would be searching for them and thus would be counted among the unemployed. For decades, the unemployment statistics have shown that while the unemployment rate for older workers is relatively low, once they become unemployed, it takes longer for them to be reemployed than for any other age group.

If the option of worklife is to be extended and practical ways found for doing so, what does this mean for education and training efforts? In what ways might organized learning be involved? What kinds of policies and experiments might we establish in the 1980s that would better prepare us for a future in which a higher and higher proportion of the population is over 60, and over 65, and over 70?

Policy Trials for the 1980s

Public and private policy on older workers and retirement has so far been concentrated in two areas. The first is income security, beginning with the Social Security Act and the development of private pensions. While incomes of many older people are far from adequate, Old Age Assistance (the welfare program) declined year after year as Social Security became more adequate. (It is now replaced by Supplemental Security, mailed with the Social Security checks, so the welfare nature of such payments has been all but eliminated.) The second thrust of public policy has been to extend medical care to older people through Medicare and Medicaid. The prospect of going without medical treatment thereby has largely been removed and the financial burden on sons and daughters relieved.

While we have gone a long way with a policy of social security, we have hardly begun on a policy of social opportunity, as we have been reminded by Willard Wirtz, who, while Secretary of Labor, wrote the 1965 *Older Worker Report,* which resulted in the Age Discrimination in Employment Act of 1967. The demands for the future are going to be more in terms of opportunity for productive activity. The timing may, in fact, be very good, for as the burden of paying for security grows, some relief may lie in more work for those who might otherwise be pushed out of the job market. There are recommended below, for further development, a number of approaches that might be tried on at least an experimental or trial basis.

In general, the strategy recommended for the 1980s is one of getting a variety of policy trials and experiments in place. Then they can be sorted through for results and practicality, and those offering the most promise can be adopted by private or public institutions, as the case may be.[8]

Workplace Demonstrations and Experiments

The most promising place to get started is at the workplace, with employers, unions, and educational institutions collaborating in carrying out a variety of efforts to deal with older worker opportunity. Some of these kinds of things are being done now in industry; they will be referred to below as examples. However, for the experience to be useful to employers and other policymakers generally, such experiments or demonstrations would have to be carefully planned and the process of carrying them out, as well as the results obtained, carefully documented in case studies for others to use.

Tapered Retirement

There is attractiveness in the logic of the proposition that as aging is a gradual process, so too could be retirement. In practice, that has not turned out to be a popular approach. But if abilities decline only slowly, why should persons be working a full schedule one week and not at all the next or evermore? There are, to be sure, complications involved, particularly in large production organizations, when people work less than full time. But there is a lot more interest today in "flexible working time" in general, and gradual retirement is only one variant of it. Twenty-five years ago, a small rubber factory in Ohio met needs for workers by allowing students to split a shift on the production line. It was a very successful arrangement for both the students and employers.

There is some limited experience with gradual retirement. In a Conference Board study published in 1977, 97 companies out of 700 surveyed had made small steps in this direction. Sixteen had increased the amount of leave during the last year or so of work, and 81 provided a shorter workweek during the last few months of work.[9] But these are very limited efforts and do not represent an extension of retirement over a long stretch of time.

A tapered arrangement could keep experienced workers at half the weekly wage cost. The idea of early retirement might be more attractive to workers if it meant starting sooner on what might be a gradual process. The link to education and work is that workers would be able to dovetail going back to the classroom or enrolling in a training institute to prepare for new occupations or "second careers." Linkages could be established with the community's education system to facilitate such arrangements for workers in gradual retirement. A few carefully documented model programs in different industries would help determine how practical and attractive this approach is and for how many workers.

Special Tuition-Aid Arrangements

Tuition-aid programs are becoming much more widespread in industry. They offer real opportunities for workers to learn new skills to help them in their quest for second careers or part-time jobs after retirement from their regular jobs. Tuition-aid programs could be made more useful as aids for employment adjustment of older workers if they were modified for this specific use. One modest possibility is, after a specified age, simply to relax normal requirements that the education or training be related to jobs within the company. Older workers could then prepare for jobs elsewhere. Another is to enlarge the benefit so that older workers could enroll over longer periods of time. Another is to couple tuition aid with paid educational leave for workers over a certain age who are preparing for new occupations. Yet another is to couple tuition aid with the tapered retirement arrangements discussed above, so that the worker would both have the time for learning and assistance with education costs.

One example of a company providing liberal assistance to help with retirement adjustment is IBM. A new retirement education assistance program, begun in 1977, provides $2,500 of education benefits ($500 per year) to workers 52 and over. The benefits can be used up to two years after retirement.[10]

Putting More In to Get More Out

To some extent there is a self-fulfilling prophecy operating that makes older workers less attractive to employers by the time they near sixty. Investments in training and retraining are heavily concentrated among the younger employees, those under 40 or 35. A combination of lack of investment in workers 40 to 55 and the fact that industrial processes change and require new skills means that older workers are often less equipped in terms of being adequately trained for new production processes than younger ones.

An older-worker program or policy in a company does not begin at age 60 or 65. To be effective, there has to be a concern with development throughout a working career. It means continuing to upgrade skills and retrain after age 40, if employers are going to get the most from workers after age 50 and 55. And if new mandatory retirement laws are such that worklife is extended, investments in the skills of workers between ages 40 and 55 may determine whether this longer worklife adds to the bottom line of the financial statement or subtracts from it.

It is, of course, not just a matter of keeping job skills up to date. Management often expresses the importance of "new blood" and motivation. Along with investment in skills go conscious efforts to keep older workers motivated and committed. Where firms continue to invest in somewhat older workers, there may well be additional payoff in the commitment older workers make to the company. And there may be other ways to refresh workers as they advance in their jobs and careers that will avoid the self-fulfilling prophecies that are neglect's result.

Part-time Jobs

There is a growing demand by older people and other groups for part-time jobs. More women are working part-time, as are high school and college students. For older workers not able to get regular full-time jobs, part-time employment is an alternative. Many, of course, would prefer such employment. In an average month, from 1 to 1.5 million persons are unemployed and seeking part-time work. Given this supply of job seekers, are there possibilities for creating more part-time employment opportunities? There are biases against the part-time employee, but little is known about whether they are justified. One example of bias is the denial of almost all fringe benefits to the part-timer. Careful investigation and experimentation might establish that this labor supply can be more profitably tapped. If it is, then links to education and training might enlarge the supply of qualified part-time workers.

One example of a firm that has permitted part-time work after regular retirement age is Continental Illinois National Bank and Trust Company. The bank has a policy of providing part-time employment to its older employees of whatever age, and the 440 older participants in the part-time program range up to 78 years of age. A Continental personnel officer reported that "with employees over 72, we ask managers to judge whether a person's health could be endangered by the work. Only twice have we had to talk to someone over 65 about leaving—both times for health reasons."[11] Can this work in other companies and industries?

Trial Retirement

If workers had the option of trying out retirement and seeing if they could make a satisfactory adjustment to another activity (such as seeking a part-time job or going back to school) while retaining the option, for some specified period, of returning to their regular jobs, they would have more flexibility in arranging second careers or seeing how they adjust to more leisure. It's hard to know what retirement is like without having a chance to try it out. The question, of course, is whether such a trial approach is consistent enough with management needs and objectives to make it feasible. The only way to find out is to try it.

Public Effort

Community-Based Job Development and Placement Efforts

While the public Employment Service has long had an older worker program, and the ES should do as much as possible to place older workers, the competition for attention at the public agency is keen and will not be sufficient to meet older worker needs. It is, therefore, important to organize efforts on older workers' behalf in the various service agencies in the community and to enlist older workers in carrying out such a program.

While such programs exist in a number of communities, many are also without them, and those programs that do exist vary greatly in their effectiveness and in the support given them. One successful and comprehensive model is Operation ABLE in Chicago. The project, organized in 1977, was an outgrowth of the effort of 20 volunteers who founded the Senior Employment Service in 1973. Finding duplication and fragmentation of services in the city, the program was reorganized as Operation ABLE. It consists of a network in Chicago of 20 independent nonprofit job agencies. Operation ABLE works to strengthen existing senior employment agencies, conducts a public awareness campaign, and does research on new work roles for adults. It also operates a centralized Job Hotline and Clearinghouse to match jobs and applicants. Just one example of a community-based service, this project was one of six community-based employment projects honored at a White House Seminar on Employment in 1978.

There needs to be a number of careful case studies of such exemplary community programs, probing the factors necessary for success, so that other communities will have the information with which to start such services.[12]

Senior Service

While it is no substitute for providing regular jobs to older people who want them, there is a basic need for productive activity of any kind, for an opportunity to make a recognized contribution. Some of this need can be met through creation of opportunities for community and public service. The tasks older people could perform in the community are endless, from school volunteer work, to meeting the growing need for child care, to creating a variety of youth programs that go beyond what government can do in CETA-type programs.

Such service programs can best be organized at the community level. While regular salaries need not be involved (unless the tasks are really those for which a public agency is responsible and the older person is in effect an employee, in which case prevailing wages should be paid), some kind of stipend arrangement would be essential. There are ample precedents for the support of such projects from the federal level in the activities of ACTION. A number of well organized and recorded Senior Community Service programs could establish both cost and practicality. Where such service workers need supplementary education or training to be able to perform the needed services, it should be built into the projects.

Activity Grants

In 1973, the Canadian government launched a project called New Horizons with an initial expenditure of $10,000. By March of 1979, Canada had spent $67 million on the program for 10,920 separate projects. According to the *Christian Science Monitor,* reporting on the program,

> Older persons won grants for doing everything from setting up old-time dances to providing kosher meals for elderly Jewish people in their homes. . . . In the province of Saskatchewan, a group harvested a grant of $15,000 to restore vintage machinery in an abandoned aircraft factory.[13]

The idea was to build on the creativity and initiative of older people, rather than to design a public program. New Horizons' grants are given only once, so after a project is underway, money has to be found elsewhere to keep it going.

Some of these projects bloomed into growing and sustained efforts. A project to offer academic courses at the university level to people over 65 has resulted in a well-subscribed continuing program and has spun off a project called Third Age Learning Associates which provides an information center where older persons can get advice about starting their own learning groups.

Would relatively small investments create substantial productive activity and needed services and products as well? There would need to be trial runs in several communities to find out.

* * * *

Work is an important part of life, and everyone gets older. It hardly makes sense in human terms for people who are living longer to be forced out of the workforce ever earlier. Kenneth Boulding has put it well: "If the young win a battle for jobs with the old, they will live to regret it."[14]

There are some hard economics involved in reversing the situation. And if people are to have second careers and extended careers, opportunity for continued education and training is also involved. The 1980s could be a time when we work out both the human factors and the economic factors. If we do, then there is still a chance that Robert Browing could be right when he wrote that, "The best is yet to be / The last of life for which the first was made."

Notes

[1] J. Roger O'Meara, *Retirement: Reward or Rejection?*, New York: The Conference Board, 1977.

[2] U.S. Department of Labor, *The Older American Report: Age Discrimination in Employment*, Report of the Secretary of Labor to the Congress, Washington, D.C.: U.S. Department of Labor, 1965, pp. 86–87.

[3] Elizabeth Meier and Elizabeth Kerr, "Capabilities of Middle-Aged and Older Workers: A Survey of the Literature," *Industrial Gerontology*, Washington, D.C., Summer, 1976, pp. 147–155.

[4] Labor force participation rates used here are from the statistical supplement to the 1977 *Employment and Training Report of the President*, pp. 142–43, for BLS Special Labor Force Report No. 218, and from *Monthly Labor Review*, February 1980.

[5] C. Rosenfeld and S. C. Brown, "The Labor Force Status of Older Workers," *Monthly Labor Review*, November 1979.

[6] T. Aldrich Finegan, *The Measurement Between Behavior and Classification of Discouraged Workers*, Background Paper No. 12, Table 3, National Commission on Employment and Unemployment Statistics, Washington, D.C., June 1978.

[7] Johnson and Higgins, Inc., "1979 Study of American Attitudes Toward Pensions and Retirement: Summary," Lou Harris and Associates, 1979, pp. vii–xiii.

[8] This goes to press just as a significant new publication has been issued, *The Future of Older Workers: New Options for an Extended Worklife*, by Jerome Rosow and Robert Zager, President and Vice-President of the Work in America Institute, Inc. Their extensive recommendations deserve careful attention by all interested in extending worklife.

[9] O'Meara.

[10] David Robison, *Training and Jobs Programs in Action*, Committee for Economic Development, in cooperation with The Work in America Institute, 1978, p. 158.

[11] Robison, p. 153.

[12] Operation ABLE, *First Annual Report*, 1977–1978.

[13] Kathleen Rex, *Christian Science Monitor*, January 28, 1980.

[14] Kenneth Boulding in a speech given at Wingspread Conference Center in 1978.

Chapter 10

Tuition Aid

Employee education isn't really a fringe benefit like health insurance or safety shoes; though clearly the employee benefits from the service. Employee education is an integral part of job growth and in the enlightened self-interest of the employer.

Polaroid Corporation

These workers are looking for an adult environment. They are threatened by being in a large, youth-oriented educational institution. So even as popular as adult education is becoming, still, when offered in the context of a youth-oriented institution, it is very alienating and threatening to a lot of workers.

Staff member, Education Fund of District Council 37, of the American Federation of State, County and Municipal Employees

We had a mandate to design the best educational plan in the U.S. We were extremely excited by the kind of commitment Kimberly-Clark was going to make as a company.

Member of design team for tuition-aid plan at Kimberly-Clark Corporation

For employees of the Polaroid and Kimberly-Clark corporations, and members of the AFSCME District Council 37, "tuition aid" is a familiar and well-used concept. For workers in these settings, the plans that provide for enrollment at educational institutions of their own choosing, and payment of tuition costs by the employer, have become a valued feature of employment.

161

For their employers, tuition aid has become an important means of developing resources needed in the workplace.

While tuition-aid arrangements are increasingly common in American industry, few are so successful (despite increasing numbers of eligible employees) as are these three programs. Yet it is possible that education funded through tuition aid will become an important stimulus to growth in education for the working population. The prospects were summed up by a recent study:

> Salted by a new employer and union interest in "tuition-aid" and worker education programs, there is prospect for a melting away of remaining barriers to bringing real educational opportunity to the adult period of life. . . . Worker education, including tuition-assistance as part of its curriculum, could be as important a development in the 1980s as the community colleges were in the 1960s—or even as the land grant colleges were a century ago.[1]

To realize the tuition-aid promise, however, requires more linkages among workers, employers, unions, and educational brokers than any other arrangement for delivering and funding education and training. On the one hand, tuition-aid arrangements are more commonplace, creating a source of funding for adult education at a time when public budgets are strained. On the other hand, worker use of these arrangements remains generally limited and educational institutions often seem ignorant of their existence. This chapter presents the known facts about tuition-aid arrangements: the extent of participation by workers; the attitudes of employers, unions, and workers toward tuition-aid plans; the barriers workers experience to using tuition aid; and practices that have proved successful. Finally, it suggests some possibilities for greater realization of the tuition-aid promise in the 1980s and beyond.

The Tuition-Aid Terrain

Although tuition aid was well established in 1957, when offered by slightly more than six out of ten firms, growth since that time has been considerable.[2] Nine out of ten United States companies with 500 or more employees offered tuition-aid benefits, according to a Conference Board study conducted in 1977.[3] While the extent has not yet been measured, many smaller companies also offered tuition aid. Among larger firms, the percentage offering tuition aid was higher, ranging from 97 percent for firms with 10,000 or more employees down to 82 percent for firms with 500 to 1,000 employees.[4]

The pattern of availability was fairly uniform across American industry except for wholesale and retail trade, where 64 percent of the larger firms (500 or more employees) had tuition aid. In all, the Conference Board study estimated that about 1.25 million employees of large firms were enrolled in tuition-aid programs in 1977; had numbers been available for the smaller firms, this total would be much higher. Even with these limited participation rates, total tuition-aid enrollment is quite large. If smaller firms could also be counted, it would probably exceed the total *full-time* enrollment in community and junior colleges, some 1.6 million students in 1979.[5]

Although most tuition-aid plans are established unilaterally by employers, growing numbers are negotiated between employers and unions. In a comprehensive study, the National Manpower Institute (now the National Institute for Work and Learning) estimated that there are 198 negotiated plans (in firms with 1,000 or more employees) covering about 1.6 million workers.[6] Whether negotiated or not, they have become standard in large firms; as one personnel officer put it, tuition-aid plans are "so fixed a feature of company policy that any abrogation or major reduction of employee rights under them is, for all practical purposes, no longer a management perogative."[7]

Principal Features of Tuition-Aid Plans

Eligibility	Most plans open to all active employees. Most require one year or less of service for eligibility.
Payment method	Employees are usually reimbursed by company after satisfactory course completion and evidence of tuition payments. Satisfactory usually means passing; sometimes it is a specific grade requirement.
Cost coverage	Plans usually cover all or part of registration fees, student activities, laboratory work, and graduation expenses. Other costs are sometimes covered: for example, books, supplies, CLEP, transportation, meals. Normally, higher payments are made for diploma or degree courses and for job-related education.
Acceptable courses	Courses must often be for credit and/or must be job-, career-, or degree-related.
Acceptable institutions	Courses frequently must be taken at colleges and universities, community colleges, technical and vocational schools, high schools, professional societies, labor unions, trade associations, or correspondence schools.
Scheduling	Most plans do not allow time off for courses, but employees often may trade shifts or adjust work schedules to accommodate courses. However, obligations to complete course work must not impair job performance.

The increasing prevalence of these tuition-aid plans has not, however, been accompanied by a rise in the rate at which eligible employees participate. On the average, only about 4 or 5 percent of workers avail themselves of this opportunity to go back to school. For hourly wage, blue-collar, and pink-collar workers, the participation rates are halved.

Plans vary with respect to the kind of courses that can be taken and amount of reimbursement. Of course, every variation may affect the extent to which each plan is utilized. The preceding table summarizes the principal features of tuition-aid plans.

The National Manpower Institute, with financing from the National Institute of Education, several years ago began an effort to find out why participation rates in education paid for by employers are so low, what kind of changes might raise participation rates, and what kinds of barriers to participation workers find. The first step was to conduct a comprehensive survey of employers, unions, and workers. The contrasts and similarities among attitudes toward tuition-aid plans elucidate many of the dynamics which continue to operate.

The NMI survey established clearly that management, unions, and workers all think tuition-aid plans have very important functions. They also have similar views as to what these functions are. The survey found that company and union officials overwhelmingly view the importance of worker education in terms of job performance, updating knowledge, and promotion and job mobility. While workers cite personal development as their prime educational objective, they also give career-related objectives high marks. Furthermore, company and union officials concur that the three most important impacts of tuition-aid plans are worker effectiveness, career development and job mobility, and job satisfaction. A large proportion of workers feel education is important for everything from improved job performance, to being a better citizen and a well-rounded person, to preparation for retirement.

Differences in perceptions begin to emerge when barriers to worker participation are considered, although even here there is more agreement than might be expected. Over 70 percent of company officials view low worker interest as the major barrier to participation in tuition-aid plans. About half thought that employees were being given insufficient encouragement by their supervisors to enroll in courses. Lack of time off for course work was cited by 41 percent of company officials, insufficient incentives by 35 percent, and lack of information about the program by 31 percent. Three-quarters of union officials, however, see problems with time off and scheduling as the major barrier, followed by lower worker interest (62 percent) and insufficient management encouragement and incentives (56 percent). The three barriers workers themselves rank the highest are insufficient management encouragement (56 percent), lack of counseling (51 percent), and lack of information about the tuition-aid plan (44 percent). Other problems workers mention relate to limited "payoff" from education, scheduling difficulties, family responsibilities, plan restrictions and red tape, and financial constraints.

Understandably, each of the three groups points to the existence of barriers resulting from conditions under the control of others. But the most striking thing is the wide area of basic agreement about the objectives of tuition-aid plans, as well as the obstacles to greater use.

The next inquiry by NMI into the dynamics of tuition-aid plans entailed substantial case studies of three plans with unusually extensive employee participation. What accounted for the very high use rates of these plans? What did companies or unions, as the case may be, do to achieve such use, and why did they try? What lessons were learned that might be applied elsewhere? The findings from three case studies of Polaroid Corporation, District 37 of AFSCME, and Kimberly-Clark are summarized below.[8]

Kimberly-Clark Corporation's Educational Opportunities Plan (EOP)

Begun in 1974, the Kimberly-Clark Educational Opportunities Plan has earned a reputation as a leader in the arena of innovative, company-sponsored tuition-assistance plans. The introduction of the comprehensive and progressive plan, which has a participation rate of over 30 percent, represented a dramatic departure from the preexisting limited and restrictive tuition-aid program, which claimed a participation rate of only 1 percent. Kimberly-Clark, headquartered in Neenah, Wisconsin, is a fast-growing, world-wide marketer of fiber-based personal care products and has been known as a corporation very advanced in human resource development.

The liberal EOP, which provides benefits to workers *and* their families for courses which do not have to be job related, is open to nearly half of the company's almost 16,000 U.S. employees. Many of the eligible employees are concentrated around Neenah, an area rich in educational institutions. Most of the eligible employees are white collar. It is also important to note that the participation rates of hourly workers under the plan are significantly lower than the overall 30-plus percent (though these rates are also significantly higher than is the norm for hourly workers). The EOP was introduced by the corporate leadership as a way to recruit, develop, and maintain a highly qualified and satisfied workforce and to evidence Kimberly-Clark's commitment to and trust in its employees. To this day, one of the most striking features of the EOP is the high degree of top-level support and enthusiasm it enjoys. Statements made by members of the initial design team still hold true:

We had a mandate to design the best educational plan in the U.S. We were extremely excited by the kind of commitment Kimberly-Clark was going to make as a company.

The plan was to be so unique and so exciting that Kimberly-Clark would be able to retain employees by offering such a benefit.[9]

The EOP includes the following major components:

- *Kim Ed Account*—a personal "bank account," determined by formula, allotted to each employee for his/her educational use. After submitting a "self-development plan," the employee may draw on this account throughout the year. The typical Kim Ed Allotment in 1978 was approximately $450. Kim-Ed includes a provision for up to ten days of educational leave per year.

- *Fam Ed Account*—financial assistance provided to employees and their families, based on a formula allotment, for current or future educational expenses. The company makes annual deposits to the account, and there are financial incentives for employees to save for the future.

- *Extended Educational Leave*—a limited number of paid leaves for up to one year. Reportedly this component of the EOP is rarely utilized.

While notable for the care and detail with which it has been designed, the EOP is also unusually flexible. Deliberate attempts have been made to include structural features which would maximize employee use of the plan. The most striking among these include:

- *liberal eligibility.* Unlike many plans, the EOP is not limited to professional or salaried employees. There is a six-month employment requirement.

- *coverage of non-job-related and cultural activities.* Again, a rarity. Courses and institutions must be approved.

- *advance payment* for tuition and other educational expenses.

- *no grade requirement or proof of course completion.*

- *unit coordinators.* In addition to full-time, high-level administration, a network of local coordinators provides crucial support services, including information on the plan and local educational opportunities.

- *considerable plan promotion and publicity,* through employee orientation, special announcements, bulletins, supervisors, and word of mouth.

Plan officials view the high participation rate as the primary indicator of EOP's success. In addition, there is other anecdotal evidence of success that supports the proposition that a well-run educational assistance plan stands to benefit employers and employees alike.

While it is impossible to determine exactly which or how many factors have led to EOP's rapid and unusual success, it appears that the plan's effectiveness can be traced to a combination of contextual and structural features. The Kimberly-Clark Educational Opportunities Plan is a carefully designed program offered to employees in an area rich in educational opportunities in a corporate context of strong support for education and self-development. Many of the plan's features directly reduce or eliminate the structural barriers which so commonly inhibit workers from using educational assistance.

The District Council 37 Education Fund

In New York City, the District Council 37 Education Fund offers an unusual array of educational programs and services to a large and diverse group of municipal employees. The Education Fund (EF) further stands out because it is union-administered in the sense that it is overseen by a board of union members and operates out of the union's headquarters. Fund programs are not only highly subscribed (the overall participation rate is about 10–12 percent and many programs reportedly have waiting lists), but they have managed to attract most heavily those groups normally viewed as least likely to take advantage of educational opportunities (low-skilled and low-paid employees).

District Council 37 (DC 37), with its over 110,000 members, is the largest council of AFSCME, the American Federation of State, County, and Municipal Employees. Known for being a progressive, service-oriented union, the Council offers a wide range of benefits for its members, including a health plan, legal services program, retirees' association, and political action program. Through an agreement negotiated in 1971, the City of New York provides $25 annually for each of over 76,000 eligible employees to be used to meet a general set of educational objectives. The total EF budget is nearly $2 million each year. The striking diversity of the Council, its membership ranging from low-paying, unskilled positions to high-paying professional ones, has been somewhat less evident in the population of Fund-eligible employees. This eligible population has included many clerical and hospital workers (often in the lower end of the pay/skill scale), while including fewer professional and blue-collar workers (frequently at the top of the skill/salary ladder). However, a new contract arrangement in 1979 made 20,000 additional employees eligible for the Fund, including many in blue-collar and professional positions, thus shifting somewhat the relative proportions among Fund-eligible employees.

As in the case of Kimberly-Clark, the top-level leadership at DC 37 has long espoused the value of education for workers. The Fund evolved out of the union leadership's attempts, in the 1960s, to meet the perceived needs of workers for education and training which would lead to job upgrading and promotional opportunities within the city's civil service system. Because of the enthusiastic response of the membership, this emphasis on career development has continued and is very evident in the focus of Fund programs today. Whether learning English, passing a civil service test, or obtaining a diploma or college degree is the immediate goal, career advancement is the primary objective of most participants.

While bargaining units of clerical and hospital workers first negotiated with the city for educational funds in 1969 (and other units subsequently did so), it was in 1971 that the DC 37 Education Fund, administered by a Board of Trustees of union members, was formally established. Prior to 1971, educational funds were administered by the city.

In an attempt to fulfill the learning needs of a very diverse population, the Fund has, over the years, developed a wide range of educational programs and offerings. Most of these offerings are in *basic skills development programs* (such as High School Equivalency, English as a Second Language, and Reading Improvement), *college degree programs* (DC 37 campuses of Hofstra University and the College of New Rochelle—not technically part of the EF, but often financed through its Tuition Refund Program—Labor/Liberal Arts for Women, and the Tuition Refund Program), and *career-related programs* (Clerical Skills, Test-Taking Preparation, Accounting, Nursing, etc.).

Key provisions and features of EF programs attempt to reduce barriers to participation in education faced by working adults who are returning to school after a long absence. These features and provisions include:

- *flexible, simplified admissions procedures,* with a minimum of the bureaucracy and red tape students reported encountering at other schools.

- *scheduling arrangements* enabling many students to attend classes on their way home from work. Most classes are held on evenings or Saturdays at union headquarters and alternative arrangements often exist to accommodate work shifts. Students gain support from attending classes with their coworkers in the union setting.

- *a diversified, nonrestrictive curriculum.* Programs are designed to meet a variety of learning needs and styles, and degree programs are not required to be job-related.

- *little or no out-of-pocket expenses for students.* The Fund is spent *only* on education programs (unlike some programs in which education is seen as a cost item for the organization sponsoring them).

- *an accessible network of support services,* including widely available group and individual educational counseling, a learning lab for tutoring and individual instruction in basic skills, a library, and a staff of faculty and administrators who reportedly often act as advisors to students.

- *widespread publicity* of the Fund and its programs, through the highly popular union newspaper, word of mouth, referrals, and notices. Especially because of the communications network, there is a high level of awareness concerning Fund programs.

Overall, the Fund is seen by the union as successful because it meets its stated objectives and succeeds in attracting large numbers of students, most of whom have positive reactions to its programs. In addition to career development, other reported major outcomes of Fund use are: improved job performance; increased self-esteem, interpersonal skills and self-confidence; improved family relations; greater readiness to pursue further education (either for personal reasons or for credentials or skills); and increased involvement in the union as a whole.

As with Kimberly-Clark, the success of the EF can be attributed to an interplay of environmental and programmatic factors. Many Fund-eligible workers have a strong, clear need for education in order to advance within the civil service system or even to maintain their jobs. Thus, when faced with a highly promoted educational program, tailored to their particular social/ psychological and learning needs and offered within a union which strongly encourages them to "own" and use such programs, many DC 37 workers choose to return to the classroom.

The Tuition Assistance Plan of Polaroid Corporation

The importance of leadership commitment and innovation emerges again in an account of the successful Tuition Assistance Plan of Polaroid Corporation. Education, creativity, and human resource development were central to the vision of Dr. Edwin Land, the founder of this successful corporation, headquartered in Cambridge, Massachusetts, an area brimming with educational opportunities. Since Land's founding of Polaroid's education program in 1957, Polaroid has placed high value on maintaining a cadre of highly trained and skilled employees who will advance throughout the Polaroid system.

As a result, the Polaroid educational program today is noted not only for its liberal Tuition Assistance Plan (TAP), but for an extensive and highly utilized internal educational and training system. The effect of all this, reports one employee, is that "education is just in the air at Polaroid." The numbers are a striking testament. Fully 50 percent of the corporation's approximately 12,000 domestic employees participated in one or more internal or external educational opportunities in 1977–78. TAP was utilized by 10 percent of the eligible workforce, and of these participants, 40 percent were hourly employees. These figures are remarkable for at least two reasons in addition to the unusually high 50 percent participation rate. First, as is the case at DC 37, TAP manages to attract significant proportions of users from the ranks of those considered least likely to utilize education and, second, TAP sustains a high level of participation despite the existence of a comprehensive internal education program.

Why does TAP do so well? Again, as was the case with the two other educational programs under study, a look at the key features of the program reveals provisions which do much to overcome some major barriers to participation.

TAP, an integrated component of the overall employee development program (which includes skills training, management and organizational development, technology-based seminars, and career counseling), exists to finance both independently undertaken external education programs as well as company-initiated programs requiring use of outside educational institutions.

Of crucial importance is the fact that TAP prepays 100 percent of costs of approved educational programs successfully completed by employees. (The money must be refunded if the employee fails to pass or complete the course.) The carefully designed plan formerly paid only partial tuition costs. Through an "equity provision," hourly and salaried employees are entitled to the same tuition assistance benefits. The corporately financed plan, with an annual budget of approximately $700,000, is open to all half- and full-time employees, with prorated assistance. Acceptable courses and programs have met criteria very broadly defined as job related. In this case, the term encompasses not only those programs related to the employee's current or future job at Polaroid, but also basic skills courses and a number of specific degree programs.

TAP is widely publicized in a variety of ways (brochures, handbooks, media, supervisors, and word of mouth) and the application process is made easy and convenient. Furthermore, not only is educational counseling made available to employees at their worksite, but it is required before financial assistance is granted. This ensures that the best educational match is made between student and course and that the objectives of both Polaroid and the employee are met.

Available anecdotal evidence from case studies suggests that the educational program at Polaroid, and its TAP component, do in fact meet their fundamental objective of promoting advancement within the company. Regular opportunities are provided for hourly employees to "break rank" and move into salaried positions, and education is reportedly the key to making this move. Whereas questions arise in many organizations regarding thwarted expectations and lack of payoff from education, at Polaroid education is not simply encouraged; it is clearly rewarded. This, in fact, appears to be an important key to TAP's success.

Again, what emerges as a recipe for success is a combination of contextual and programmatic features. Counseling, publicity, full prepayment, and simplified, liberal requirements and procedures all tailor the plan to the needs of working adults. Furthermore, Polaroid, from its highest leadership levels through the rest of its staff, has exhibited a clear and continuing commitment to the education and human development of all its employees. What Edwin Land envisioned decades ago is still in the air at Polaroid.

* * * *

Taken together, these three case studies suggest ways to bridge the gap between positive attitudes toward education and underutilized tuition-aid plans. At Kimberly-Clark, District Council 37, and Polaroid, similar sets of structural barriers were consciously diminished or removed, with the result that all three plans have since elicited high employee interest and use. Introducing the following features into a tuition-aid plan need not be difficult and could go a long way toward promoting greater use:

- little or no out-of-pocket expense to the worker

- broad eligibility within the firm

- simplified admissions and approval procedures

- broad range of allowable courses

- widespread publicity and information about the plan

However, another set of factors is clearly in evidence at all three sites. Their relative importance in breeding success cannot be known with certainty, although each contributes to the contextual environment at these sites. These factors include:

- top-level leadership belief in and endorsement of education

- institutional support for education at all levels

- "payoffs" from the use of education which are either clearly evident to workers or strongly needed and sought

One must be cautious, however, in drawing inferences and implications from these case studies. First, a sampling of three is hardly large enough to establish firm conclusions. Much more testing and study is needed. Further, the case-study method does not allow for the isolation and testing of the relative influence of different variables. The three case studies do not shed light on the relative importance of the various factors presumed responsible for enhancing participation. How many are needed to make a program work? Also, even at these three "successful" sites, the proportion of workers who utilize the educational assistance available to them is still much less than the overall proportion who profess a belief in the importance of education.

The NMI study sums up the implications which can be drawn from the three programs:

> What emerges from the three programs is the broad common instruction that if the employee education idea is taken seriously, if tuition assistance is made part of a broader education and training program, if provision is made for a staff function adequate to supply initiative which is apparently not going to develop among very many employees individually—then a substantial degree of participation, with apparently significant consequences, will result. . . . It is essential to recognize, too, that all three of these cases involve sufficiently large groups of employees to warrant the development of broad-gauge, well-staffed programs. These programs suggest strongly the advantages that accrue from making a tuition-aid plan one part of a broad employee education and training curriculum. Yet to list the principal characteristics of these particular initiatives is to realize that virtually all of them suggest smaller scale and partial replications.[10]

Experimenting with Improvement

The NMI survey of employers, union, and workers, and the three case studies, identify several distinct barriers to participation, as well as avenues for enlarging opportunity. Some of these barriers have to do with the basic features of the plan itself, others with implementing the plan so that employees can take maximum advantage of it. By analyzing all available information, NMI distilled three straightforward approaches to implementation that confront the major barriers to tuition-aid use. Three experiments are underway to test how much each additional step changes participation in the plan.

These three experimental demonstrations are designed to provide for a testing and isolation of variables that was not possible during the case studies. Three worksites are involved at which labor and management officials have a joint interest in raising the level of worker participation in their education plans. The year-long projects began in 1979. At the time of this writing, these experiments are still in process so it is not yet known what changes have occurred as a result of the interventions. What follows is a brief profile of each project, including its current status. The profile is adapted from a description of the demonstration projects prepared by NMI staff carrying out the Worker Education and Training Project.

Model 1—Information Delivery

This demonstration project of the Communications Workers of America, Local 11588, and General Telephone of California, Pomona, California, is designed to provide information to some 1,800 hourly workers at several General Telephone Company (GTC) of California plants in the Pomona area. Since half of the workers surveyed by NMI said they knew nothing about their tuition-aid plans, providing such information seemed a good place to start. Through joint efforts by GTC and the Communications Workers of America, Local 11588, workers are being given information about the company's tuition assistance plan and local education and training opportunities.

One-on-one contacts by ten worker-members of the project's Education Committee and group meetings of workers sponsored by both the union and the company are being used as an initial means of introducing the workers to the idea of participating in education. The committee members' basic functions are to meet with the employees and to apprise them of the existence and nature of their tuition-aid plan and the available educational opportunities within the area. As of February 1980, each of the employees in the target group has been contacted, either one-to-one by a committee member or as part of a small group. The committee has started contacting the employees a second time. They will again inform, motivate, stimulate, and encourage each to return to school and use tuition-assistance benefits. Committee members meet weekly with the Site Coordinator to discuss the program and problems and to compare notes from contacts made during the week.

In addition to personal contacts, other means are employed on-site to broadcast information on educational opportunities. These methods include bulletin board posters, letters to each employee in the target group, handout folders, and articles in company and union publications.

Model 2—Information Delivery and Educational Advisement

The Model 2 demonstration project is to be attempted in Cleveland, Ohio, at Local 18 of the International Union of Operating Engineers (IUOE). Initial development work is underway. This model is designed to do two things:

1. *to provide information* on Local 18's training site programs and facilities, its Education and Safety Fund (tuition assistance for members), and educational opportunities in the Cleveland area; and, beyond this,

2. *to establish an on-site education advisement* capability for members by training a number of Local 18 stewards as Education Information Advisors (EIAs).

The Site Coordinator and EIAs are currently working to develop and publicize the union-sponsored GED program to be held at the union hall. The program is being sponsored by the union for the membership who will be able to use tuition assistance money from their Education and Safety Fund to cover the costs of participation and testing. This program and others which are developed as a result of this project will be publicized through the Local 18 newspaper and by special bulletins and handouts from the union.

In addition to this activity, work is underway to develop a section on educational opportunity and advising for the IUOE stewards' training manual for use by EIAs at the site. EIAs will be provided with information on union-sponsored classes, training site hours and equipment, and local schools' course schedules to use on-site in advising their fellow members.

Model 3—Information, Advisement, and Improved Delivery of Educational Options

Model 3 is a joint demonstration project among the State of Connecticut, two unions representing state workers—the Connecticut State Employees Association (CSEA) and the Connecticut Employees Union Independent (CEUI) —and the Coordinating Committee for the North Central Region (CCNCR), which consists of higher education institutions. This model, in addition to providing information and advisement services, is designed also to *improve delivery of education options* based on workers' expressed needs at the site. Five state agencies are participating in the demonstration project, targeted to reach some 500 workers in both the clerical and the maintenance bargaining units.

Eleven Education Information Advisors (EIAs) representing state workers from both bargaining units are currently collecting and disseminating information and advising their coworkers on available educational opportunities. To date, methods used to reach employees include large group meetings sponsored by agencies, small group meetings arranged by EIAs, one-to-one contacts between EIAs and their coworkers, development of agency-specific posters for bulletin boards, articles in the *State Scene* newspaper and in the union papers, and handouts on the projects. While the Connecticut demonstration is similar to those in California and Ohio in its information delivery aspects, the Connecticut model's design also includes a consortium of educational institutions on the project's local planning committee to facilitate delivery of educational programming to target group workers.

The GM-UAW Experiment

An experiment somewhat similar to the above three now being carried out by NMI was an attempt, over a decade ago, to raise participation in a tuition refund program negotiated between General Motors (GM) and the United Auto Workers (UAW).[11] The experiment, carried out at a Cleveland plant with 3,000 employees, was launched as a cooperative labor-management project in 1965. Since the refund program's introduction in 1964, only five employees had made use of it.

The experiment involved establishing a branch of a private technical school at the union hall, only a few blocks from the factory. The UAW publicized the school, and its local Education Committee helped students with applications and processing, aided recruitments, and provided tutoring. Classes were offered before and after work shifts. By 1967, over 150 employees had attended the school. In 1966, GM launched a company-wide publicity campaign, involving supervisors and foremen, to acquaint workers with all facets of the tuition refund program. Increased interest led to creation of an educational information center in the plant cafeteria. Though younger employees often utilize educational benefits for job advancement, many older workers at the Cleveland plant return to school simply for intellectual satisfaction. Again, information, counseling, improved linkages between schools and the workplace, and institutional support for education were identified as factors raising participation in education.

From Experience

A careful sifting of experience with tuition-aid plans, from both employer and worker perspectives, leads to several approaches very likely to raise employee participation in education programs. There is no way to quantify the value of each approach, or to know exactly what combination of approaches will accomplish the most for the least cost. But each company, union, or employee organization will have judgments about which are likely to work best in their own environments. In no particular order of priority, the approaches are described below.

Adequate Information

It is obvious that workers who don't know the provisions of their tuition-aid plan will not take advantage of it. Yet, about half of the eligible workers surveyed by NMI (now NIWL) do not know about their plan. Companies with high participation rates have made deliberate efforts to get the word out through various means. Unions can do this also.

Adequate Counseling and Advisement

Employees need someone to talk to who can help them with their educational plans, and explain exactly what is available in the community. One approach is to train a few workers, union shop stewards, or individuals in the personnel office for this role. At one project, these counselors are called Education Information Advisors, and at another, Learning Organizers. Or alternatively, a small amount of money could be authorized under the tuition-aid plan to pay for such counseling services from the growing network of Educational Brokering Centers in the community.

Minimal Out-of-Pocket Costs

When workers do not have to pay the tuition cost in advance they are more likely to participate, and the plans reviewed by NMI with the highest participation rates entail little or no out-of-pocket costs. This can be done by advancing the money for tuition rather than reimbursing workers for it afterward. If that is not possible, money could be loaned at a low interest rate. Efforts also could be made to get the educational institution to allow payment on an installment plan.

Responsiveness of Educational Institutions

If participation is to grow, and if enrollments at educational institutions are to grow thanks to this source of private funding, educational institutions will have to go to the employees to find out what courses are wanted. Since so many adults had unhappy experiences with education when young and retain fears about returning to regular classrooms, educators may need to offer more instruction at the worksite, union hall, or some other setting in which workers are comfortable.

Large Range of Approved Courses

There will be some debate among employers as to what kinds of courses should be reimbursed. Some employers require that courses be related to the current job. An increasing number require only that education be related to some job in the company. Kimberly-Clark has no such limitation at all. And, of course, the term job-related leaves a lot of room for choice depending on how broadly it is defined by employers.

How each employer defines limits on what courses can be taken will depend on what objectives have been set for the company's tuition-aid plan. But whether workers take greater advantage of tuition-aid opportunities will depend a great deal on eligibility for a broad array of courses.

Attitude Toward Education

Whether or not workers have enthusiasm for education will be partially determined by something as real as it is intangible: whether the management communicates a belief that education is good for workers and good for the company. At Polaroid "education is in the air," and if it is highly valued elsewhere, that company's employees will also feel it.

Collaboration

It is much more likely that tuition-aid opportunities on paper will be converted to real educational activity if the employers, unions, workers, and educators collaborate in working out problems, in getting advice to workers, and in getting the right courses offered at the right times and in the right places. Particularly useful vehicles for such collaboration are the Community Education Work Councils springing up in many places, which represent all these sectors. But the main thing is that these parties get together, through whatever forum, because connections must be made between these key sectors if a better connection is to be made between education and the workplace.

A Tuition Assitance Service

The experiences described here, and the policies suggested for consideration relate to private institutions, for tuition aid is an educational development almost wholly confined to the private sector. One need, however, goes beyond plan-by-plan and community-by-community considerations. The private sector needs a service that would get information about the best practices to employers, unions, and educational institutions, and one that would facilitate the spread of successful experiences. It would help educational institutions understand how they can increase their enrollments; employers, how they might best meet their human resource development needs; and unions, how they can better help members avail themselves of educational opportunities, all through tuition aid. A Tuition Assistance Service that could gain the confidence of private institutions, and help facilitate—through information and technical assistance—an opportunity for the fuller development of human resources at the workplace could answer this need.

* * * *

Tuition aid is almost as little known as it is pervasive, almost as neglected as it is acclaimed by its creators, and almost as important—if it were more fully developed—as the educational movement that brought community and junior colleges into existence. It sits there, almost sleeping, as educators and public servants search for "lifelong learning," so far only a fetching phrase in search of a meaning. The future of the learning society may well lie, in large part, in waking this sleeping giant.

Notes

[1] Willard Wirtz, *Tuition-Aid Revisited: Tapping the Untapped Resource,* National Manpower Institute, Washington, D.C., 1979, pp. 1, 31.

[2] Bureau of National Affairs, *Tuition-Aid Plans for Employees,* Personnel Policies Forum Survey No. 299, Washington, D.C., 1975.

[3] Seymour Lusterman, *Education in Industry,* New York: The Conference Board, 1977, p. 32.

[4] Lusterman.

[5] Community and junior college enrollment estimates are from the *1980 Community, Junior, and Technical College Directory,* American Association of Community and Junior Colleges, Washington, D.C., p. 2.

[6] Ivan Charner et al., *An Untapped Resource: Negotiated Tuition-Aid in the Private Sector,* National Manpower Institute, Washington, D.C., p. 27.

[7] Lusterman.

[8] These summaries are drawn from the three case studies published by the National Manpower Institute in 1979. They are *Polaroid Corporation's Tuition Assistance Plan,* by Kathleen Knox; *The Education Fund of District Council 37,* by Jane Shore; and *Kimberly-Clark Corporation's Educational Opportunities Plan,* by Leslie Rosow.

[9] Leslie A. Rosow, *Kimberly-Clark Corporation's Educational Opportunities Plan: A Case Study,* National Manpower Institute, Washington, D.C., 1979, p. xii.

[10] Wirtz, pp. 28, 30.

[11] Max Shoenfeld, "Labor, Management Join to Stimulate Education," *Adult Learning,* May 1967.

Chapter 11

More Distant Shores

Water dissolves wood and stone and salt; air dissolves water; electric fire dissolves air; but the intellect dissolves fire, gravity, laws, in its resistless menstruum. . . . Intellect is the simple power anterior to all action or construction.

Ralph Waldo Emerson, 1841

A summary of any book runs the risk of being gratuitous to someone who has read it and a misrepresentation to someone who has not. No summary of this book will be attempted. However, it may be useful to review our central purposes and to place our effort in the context of what may lie ahead.

Each chapter of this book has enlarged upon the premise that there are learning connections to many of the transitions we make and goals we pursue during our adult and worklives: adaptations to a changing society and economy, adjustments enabling our economic system to deal with declining productivity and increasing competition in foreign markets, our society's pursuit of the twin objectives of increased equality and greater opportunity, and the struggle to make the best use of our lives.

Although many learning opportunities currently exist for people whose education ceased when they were young, information about these opportunities is scattered and incomplete. If American society seriously intends to become more systematic about organized learning during adult life, one indication would be a decision to periodically measure adult participation in learning on a much broader basis than is now the case.

Opportunities for organized learning exist in many more and diverse locations than are conjured up by the familiar image of a classroom in a formal educational institution. Organized learning for adults takes place through elementary schools, vocational and technical institutions, community and junior colleges, four-year colleges and universities, special weekend colleges for adults, off-campus learning sites, industry classrooms and on-the-job training, joint labor-management apprenticeship programs, union-created courses and educational institutions, industry tuition-aid arrangements, correspondence programs, professional organizations, formal educational arrangements offered over television, county agricultural extension agencies, YMCAs, churches, and many other places as well. We believe that the broad range of adult needs is served by building on this diversity rather than by searching for a single, uniform approach.

The patterns of participation in adult learning vary among different population groups, and reveal that those with the most education as young people tend to take most advantage of learning opportunities as adults. A series of measures are advanced in this book to remove the barriers to learning faced by many and to promote equality of opportunity even as new opportunities are increased.

Industry sponsors a much more extensive education and training system than is generally recognized, offering college- and graduate-level instruction in corporation classrooms, structured and informal on-the-job training, and a broad range of short-term formal instruction, including everything from leadership development to job skill training to safety training. Industry training is vital to the industrial process, but remains generally unknown outside of individual corporations; virtually no comprehensive and systematic effort has been made, either inside or outside of industry, to evaluate the effect of training and education investments on industrial productivity. Nor does it help that industry education/training systems and educational institutions (secondary and postsecondary) seldom communicate or work with each other.

Until corporations pay more attention to training and education in terms of its effect on output, little basis will exist for rational determinations of the optimum levels for training and educational investments. If we had measures of such investment in all industries, individual firms could compare their own investments. Any such measurements, however, should be carried out with the participation of the employer and, where applicable, union representatives to make it truly useful to decision-makers.

Organized labor in the United States has had a strong interest in education from the beginning and has consistently supported public education. Unions are active in education and training on many fronts and frequently cooperate with higher education institutions to expand opportunities. Despite this commitment, there is tension between unions and the educational establishment. Part of this tension derives from a union belief that higher education neither tries to enlarge learning opportunities for workers nor consults at the outset with unions on new educational ventures. The failure to have union representation on the first Career Education Advisory Committee, appointed by the White House in the early 1970s, is an example of this neglect.

No doubt organized labor will continue to press for expanded learning opportunity for workers. Labor could contribute significantly to the 1980s by training many more "learning organizers"—workers, union members, or officers who serve as brokers between workers and educational establishments by providing information and helping them match their talents to the community's educational institutions.

Ensuring that "educational brokering" services, which match adults desiring further education with opportunities, are widely available is essential if opportunity is to be expanded and the present pattern of participation favoring the better educated is to be broken. This can be accomplished by expanding the number of free-standing brokering services, improving the capacity of the Employment Service, CETA offices, and neighborhood associations for counseling and information dissemination, and specifying in public education ways and means to ensure that everyone knows about and has access to learning opportunities.

Another learning connection is evident in the situation of older workers who prefer productive activity to retirement. The 1980s will probably see, as a result of inflation, a reexamination of the early retirement policy, changes in mandatory retirement laws, changes in the Social Security system's financial burdens, and the substantial increase in the older population. Whether an older worker is retraining to stay with an employer or preparing for a second or third career, education and training are required in conjunction with other new arrangements for tapered retirement, trial retirement, and more generous tuition-aid benefits.

Tuition-aid programs in the private sector, through which the employer pays the costs of going to school, are now available to tens of millions of employees, and growing. Yet surprisingly, many higher education institutions, as well as a large percentage of employees covered, are unaware of these plans and the eligibility requirements.

Concentrated study of tuition aid by the National Institute for Work and Learning, from 1976 to 1980, through surveys, case studies, demonstrations, and policy explorations, has established that proper attention to these programs could realize their great promise for funding adult learning in the 1980s. From the NIWL study come a number of specific recommendations for employers, unions, and educators, including the establishment of a tuition-aid service to help these employers, educational institutions, and unions move forward on the tuition-aid front.

Among other institutions, two-year community colleges—which spearheaded adult learning in the 1970s—and four-year colleges and universities have a base of experience that will enable them to become more widely available for adult and working populations. Although these institutions enter the 1980s with greater experience in adult learning, many remain imbued with the purposes and practices of traditional college-age education, rather than new philosophies and objectives for adult learning. Labels for adult learning such as "nontraditional" tell us more about what learning is not than what it is.

As the quantity of postsecondary learning opportunity is augmented, equal attention to quality and maintenance of standards is essential, particularly as some institutions try to compensate for a shortage of younger students by entering the adult market unprepared to deliver appropriate education. Another quality problem will be in taking advantage of technological achievements such as television and satellites while instructional content to feed into these technologies remains very underdeveloped.

There is one area of worklife education and training in particular that is of top priority as we enter the 1980s. Workers find themselves buffeted by the kinds of economic changes resulting from high energy costs, increased imports of manufactured goods, and recessions brought on to help cool inflationary fires. Many of these workers will need to learn new skills so that they can switch to growing industries. Helping workers make such occupational adjustments is preferable to the rigidities and costs involved in preventing change, and we could not stop many changes even if we wanted to.

We have had some experience in using training to help workers make occupational transitions under the 1962 Manpower Development and Training Act. Cash assistance is being provided for import-connected unemployment under the Trade Adjustment Assistance program, but very few workers are getting new skills under that program. Help under CETA is postponed until the situation gets bad enough that the worker meets the means test—until despair has already set in. We need to fashion an Occupational Adjustment Assistance effort, working with employers, unions, educators, and government.

Policy directions for the early 1980s can proceed from well-established beachheads, for in all cases, there is a base of experience to build upon, and a reasonable degree of consensus concerning basic objectives. The purpose of writing this book has been to identify practical courses for private and public decision-makers to take, based on these beachheads, and remaining within this basic consensus.

Underlying this purpose is the belief that we will move forward by building upon what exists in the adult learning enterprise, rather than by tearing down the old and constructing wholly new edifices based on the logic of detached cerebral processes. This means accepting diversity, uneven growth, and accommodation between divergent individual and institutional interests.

Although the preceding chapters propose substantial changes, only the possible and the reasonable are recommended. These are essentially modest suggestions, proposed against a backdrop of renewed commitment to organized learning during worklife and the development of the mind as a central aspect of adult life.

Implementation of these modest proposals, early in this decade, would place the adult learning enterprise in a more strategic position from which to realize an even greater commitment through learning to the fuller development of human potential and increased economic growth. What would then be required are less modest steps to accelerate development of the learning enterprise. These steps could include:

- Designing a "paid educational leave" to permit employees time for education like that provided through the college or university sabbatical. Figuring out the details of paying for sabbaticals will require cooperation among industry, government, and workers.

- Making adult education "entitlements" more universally available. This is beginning to happen as the federal Basic Education Opportunity Grants and related programs are liberalized.

- Striking agreements among industry, organized labor, and government concerning a policy to encourage private investment in workplace training and education and to ensure that the *skill* component of productivity (of which there are many components) is fully realized. One concept, the Human Investment Tax Credit, parallels in theory the Investment Tax Credit for plant and equipment. It will be necessary, however, to recognize the different needs among industries. Moreover, corporate management will have to accord industrial skill development the importance now accorded to marketing and finance.

- Developing a full-fledged national (not simply federal) occupational change adjustment program to prevent workers from being wrecked on the shoals of economic changes necessary for the nation. To succeed, the program would require tripartite governance by government, industry, and unions.

- Offering workers the option of education and skill improvement instead of only idleness and unemployment insurance during recessions. Again, industry, organized labor, and government would share responsibility for working out practical approaches.

- Encouraging a sincere commitment to equality for adults in postsecondary education, rather than the common attitude that adult learning exists to generate revenue now that youth enrollments are declining.

- Establishing Work-Education Councils, composed of employers, unions, educators, local governments, service organizations, and responsible citizens, in *every* community in the nation, as was recently recommended by the Carnegie Council on Higher Education, chaired by Clark Kerr.

After these additional steps, the learning society would have become a visible counterpoint and complement to the goods-producing society for which the United States is famous. We say complement, because learning is an essential precondition for any society hoping to remain competitive in the world economy.

The recommendations made in the body of this book are modest steps about which there is considerable consensus. Above are a few more venturesome steps toward a learning society which would further the goals of developing the human potential and assisting the goods-producing society during this time of difficulty. There is a third perspective from which to view enlarged opportunity throughout working life, and that is whether a learning connection is inherent in the transition underway in mature industrial economies. In the long run, we look forward to the necessity of interpreting growth in a new way, or at least more broadly, than by the Gross National Product. On the one hand, U.S. production of goods is increasingly constrained, a fact sufficiently well recognized to eliminate the need for a litany of the industrial economy's woes, reaching from the fossil fuel shortage to inflation. On the other hand, our very success in production has left us with a yearning for something more, a yearning not satisfied by a third car or an automatic garage door. It is a yearning for clearer purpose.

It is important to ask whether a much-expanded adult learning structure could help during the profound transitions underway in economy and society. One heralded sign of transition is the expansion of the service sector of the economy in comparison with the goods-producing sector. This trend is not only decades old, but it shows every sign of continuing.

The importance of this change is not only its impact upon economic productivity, traditionally sluggish in the service sector, but also the meaning of an economy based on people serving other people, rather than people relating chiefly to machines, especially those machines that require fewer and fewer people. A people-to-people base for an economy seems not at all frightening, and may offer at least as much promise from the standpoint of the worker of fulfilling human purpose as the producing of goods. What we do not yet know is how a predominant service sector will affect our standard of living as we now define it by per capita income. For example, the bank teller learning about investments and money markets has exciting prospects compared to what the assembly-line worker can see ahead in terms of challenge and opportunity; moreover, the teller's working surroundings are usually more pleasant. However, the assembly-line worker earns twice as much money as the bank teller and the ratio of tellers to bank presidents is not very favorable. Nor do we know how many cars we must sell at home and abroad for there to be enough money in those banks.

So there remain questions about what the transition to a service-dominated economy will mean. But we know that it is underway and has positive aspects as well as possible threats to traditional economic growth. A growing learning sector would be both one aspect of the growing human services sector and also a means of equipping people for new kinds of worklife and career paths.

Another important transition long underway is the tendency of the larger economic organizations (those with better-paying jobs, fringes, reasonable stability, and other bonuses) to be able to meet production goals with fewer of the oldest and youngest people. We have an unemployment problem among 60- to 75-year-olds and among people in the youngest working years. Numerous structural adjustments are recommended in this book to increase productive opportunity later in life, but there is a limit to what can be done if the economy does not sustain enough jobs.

Meeting the job demands of women pouring into the labor force is a similar challenge. The impressive quantitative increase in the employment of women has obscured the fact that it is concentrated in lower-paying jobs in the service sector; the occupational profiles of men and women remain disparate. And, of course, long-excluded minorities also demand increased occupational opportunities.

At a time when the industrial economy is suffering under increasing constraints to traditional growth, there are now new demands for jobs whose quality is defined in traditional terms. There will, of course, be new ways to deal with the fossil fuel shortages and inflation that limit this traditional economic growth, but the days when the Gross National Product could soar without inhibition are probably behind us. Yet employment expectations still soar, and therein lies a dilemma.

Can enlarged learning opportunity help ease this worsening mismatch between expectations and opportunities? Would greater time spent in education, retraining, and skill upgrading on the part of the prime working force (say between 25 and 55) increase the number of work stations to meet the new demands of women, minorities, and older people? Can learning opportunities steer this expanded labor force into the new areas opening in the service sector and avoid the disappointment of knocking on closed factory doors? Can more people learn how to be entrepreneurs in the people sector, to take advantage of new opportunities for services delivery, from tutoring to child care centers? Is this a renewed opportunity for small businesses with limited investment capital?

There may be another transition underway, one that will transform our definition of productive roles in the society and economy. Have we defined our identities and measured our own worth too much according to the status of paid employment in the industrial economy? As important as traditional modes of success are, are there no other outlets for the desire to contribute? How are we to face the societal dissension inevitable as these traditional opportunities diminish relative to the demand? If society values the continued development of the mind, the enhancing of skills, and the transfer to all citizens of the knowledge hidden in books and the minds of a few, then the pursuit of learning itself will become a "productive" role, and offer greater opportunity for employment in the learning industry at the same time. Expanded learning opportunity may in this way further our transition from uninhibited GNP growth to a new kind of growth.

So it is appropriate to ask not simply whether the modest steps proposed in this book are useful for the reasons suggested, or whether an acceleration of these steps could help society meet traditional objectives, but also whether learning can help society negotiate the major transitions necessary if we are to adapt to the reality of limited energy sources and an aging industrial economy, while discovering new ways of growing as a society.

Americans do not want to settle either for winding down the industrial economy or for any pallid substitute for the growth that produced the two-car garage. This country has always been growing on one front or another. This is the same spirit that inspired the first immigrants and the settling of the western frontier, until Frederick Jackson Turner announced in the 1890s its closing. Now the frontier of the Gross National Product has a finite future. We cannot continue manufacturing more, bigger, and faster things indefinitely.

But there is a new frontier: the continued development of the mind, a frontier well explored if not yet accurately mapped. This frontier is in the mainstream of human evolution, and offers unlimited possibilities. Indeed, it is the mind, well-educated and developed, which will lead us onward to new frontiers of human purpose and meaning as well as restore our eminence in the world marketplace. The learning connections explored in these pages are possibilities which may contribute to progress toward the twin American objectives of expanded opportunity and increased equality, as society searches for continued growth and renewed definition.

But the GNP has long been recognized as a one-dimensional measure of growth, and to accept the GNP as the sole criterion for *Homo sapiens'* progress would be to diminish the future of our society and our children.

Index

About the Author

PAUL BARTON is Vice President for Planning and Policy Development at the National Institute for Work and Learning in Washington, D.C. Previously he has worked in the Executive Office of the President (now the Office of Management and Budget) as well as the Department of Labor with responsibility for such areas as employment and training policy, vocational education, and the relationship between manpower policy and economic policy. Mr. Barton holds a baccalaureate degree from Hiram College and a Masters in Public Affairs from Princeton University.